SEX AND THE
CITY OF GOD

A Memoir of Love and Longing

Carolyn Weber

An imprint of InterVarsity Press
Downers Grove, Illinois

InterVarsity Press
P.O. Box 1400, Downers Grove, IL 60515-1426
ivpress.com
email@ivpress.com

InterVarsity Press® is the book-publishing division of InterVarsity Christian Fellowship/USA®, a movement of students and faculty active on campus at hundreds of universities, colleges, and schools of nursing in the United States of America, and a member movement of the International Fellowship of Evangelical Students. For information about local and regional activities, visit intervarsity.org.

All Scripture quotations, unless otherwise indicated, are taken from The Holy Bible, New International Version®, NIV®. Copyright © 1973, 1978, 1984, 2011 by Biblica, Inc.™ Used by permission of Zondervan. All rights reserved worldwide. www.zondervan.com. The "NIV" and "New International Version" are trademarks registered in the United States Patent and Trademark Office by Biblica, Inc.™

While any stories in this book are true, some names and identifying information may have been changed to protect the privacy of individuals.

Cover design and image composite: Cindy Kiple
Interior design: Daniel van Loon
Images: man and woman holding hands: © Anthony Garcia / EyeEm / Getty Images
cityscape: © Jackal Pan / Moment Collection / Getty Images

ISBN 978-0-8308-4585-9 (print)
ISBN 978-0-8308-4384-8 (digital)

Printed in the United States of America ∞

InterVarsity Press is committed to ecological stewardship and to the conservation of natural resources in all our operations. This book was printed using sustainably sourced paper.

Library of Congress Cataloging-in-Publication Data
A catalog record for this book is available from the Library of Congress.

P 25 24 23 22 21 20 19 18 17 16 15 14 13 12 11 10 9 8 7 6 5 4 3 2 1

Y 41 40 39 38 37 36 35 34 33 32 31 30 29 28 27 26 25 24 23 22 21 20

Kent's again, of course,

and Hope's

The fig tree forms its early fruit;
the blossoming vines spread their fragrance.

Arise, come, my darling;
my beautiful one, come with me.

SONG OF SONGS 2:13

And thus it has come to pass, that though there are very many
and great nations all over the earth, whose rites and customs,
speech, arms, and dress are distinguished by marked differences,
yet there are no more than two kinds of human society, which
we may justly call two cities, according to the language of our
Scriptures. The one consists of those who wish to live after the
flesh, the other of those who wish to live after the spirit; and
when they severally achieve what they wish, they live in peace,
each after their kind.

SAINT AUGUSTINE, CITY OF GOD

These days, everyone has friends and colleagues; no one
really has lovers—even if they have slept together.

CANDACE BUSHNELL, SEX AND THE CITY

CONTENTS

IN ANTICIPATION

*I have read in Plato and Cicero sayings that are very wise
and very beautiful; but I never read in either of them,
"Come unto me, all ye that labor and are heavy laden."*

St. Augustine

A brain bleed seems far from a racy start to a book with the word "sex" in its title. Yet start here I will, as it is customary of epics to begin *in medias res,* or "in the middle of things," and art is symbolic of interior life. As Swede Land, sister to the protagonist of Leif Enger's beautiful novel *Peace Like a River,* asks: "Is it hubris to believe we all live epics?" I wonder: Is it hubris to believe we do not?

I received the call from the hospital while prying from my limbs sticky children slurping the last of their popsicles. My elderly father had just arrived by ambulance, the ER nurse informed me. "It appears he fell in his bathroom," she explained. When I asked how he was doing, the nurse said it would be best if the doctor spoke with me. I waited a few moments while she passed the phone to a voice who identified herself as the intern. She told me that they were assessing my father's situation, but that she was not yet at liberty to say anything else.

"Is he okay?" I asked. "I mean, is he conscious? Is he seriously hurt?" Again, the intern asserted that she could not make any decisive evaluations.

"He seems stable. I wouldn't worry just yet," she assured me in an authoritative voice. "But he is having trouble communicating."

That would be my dad, having trouble communicating, I couldn't help but think wryly to myself. My dad could be a wildcard in the communication department at the best of times.

"I will be there shortly," I spoke calmly into the phone.

"We have things under control here," the intern replied. "There is nothing you can do for him at the moment. He is comfortable. Feel free to call back for an update until you can make it in."

I thanked her and hung up. I was concerned and moved around to get ready to leave, but I was not in a mad rush. My father had fallen several times before, and he was the quintessential difficult patient: stubborn and wary, a ruthless combination. I was sure once he got his bearings back, he'd get his communication in good order too, and start giving those nurses hell—well, maybe not the pretty ones.

A few times now I had dropped everything to race out after such a call from the hospital, only to find him charming the nurses and complaining about how his legs gave out without warning, but refusing to accept any help. There he'd be when I swept in, propped up on his hospital cot and cutting me off from even saying hello with a quick finger against his lips while he made a cuckoo sign with the other hand next to his head and nodding at the incoherent patient in the bed next to him.

So this time I decided to move more methodically, taking my time in preparation to do battle with him at length. It would be tough to convince him that he needed to accept more help now. I sighed and wiped little faces and hands, and sent the older children out the door while I searched for my wallet and keys. It was an unseasonably warm, even muggy, autumn day, and the children lingered in the yard, reluctant to return to school following the lunch break. I would have to gather them and get them back, a feat much like herding cats, then hand over the toddler to my husband, Kent, who worked from home. Oh yes, I better put gas in the car on the way . . . and send a quick text to my brother and sister saying that I could deal with this while they were at work and I would fill them in later tonight . . . and maybe I should throw some coffee in a travel mug? I was so tired from being up with our littlest one the night before . . .

Something rumbled, far off, so faintly at first I wasn't sure I had even sensed it. Then, yes, there it was: thunder rose and fell in the distance. Unusual, I noted, for October. The phone rang again.

"Mrs. Weber?" the same ER nurse's voice spoke in my ear.

"Yes?" I replied. Even though the kitchen felt close in this unexpected fall heat, something in her tone shot icicles into my fingertips.

"I would come right away," she said in an urgent, low voice.

"But I thought the doctor said there was ample time yet . . . I thought you couldn't give an opinion," I stammered.

"Something has . . ." she took a breath and then breathed the next word out heavily: "changed."

In turn, I felt the air go out of me. "Oh," I exhaled.

"If it were my father, I would want to come right away," she added gently.

"Ah, yes, I see," I managed to croak past a sudden lump in my throat. "Thank you; thank you so much for calling."

Everything seemed to spin and go still at the same time. Thunder tumbled more loudly in the distance, a great surf coming in.

Oh Father, Great Artificer, what embroidery of grace could possibly lurk here?

.ılılıllııı.

My keys lay on the table amid the pictures I had been scrapbooking with the kids. We were putting the photos together for Grandpa, an early Christmas gift. As I go to scoop up my keys, one of my childhood photos catches my eye. Seeing the image transports me to the past as I move toward the car.

Suddenly I'm at my seventh birthday party. I beam up at the camera over a simple cake marked by a Pink Panther candle. I can still remember that Pink Panther candle; in my mind's eye, it made the entire occasion special. Such a winsome light dancing upon an otherwise unassuming slab of vanilla! The cartoon figure of the Pink Panther slinks its slender body around the number seven, curling its tail around the years of my life and debonairly tipping its hat toward the birthday bearer. "Here's to you," he seems to say with rosy cheer.

In the photo, my younger sister, her broken arm bound in a sling close to her chest, looks less impressed but still excited. Having toppled from a chair at our lemonade stand the week before, her look betrays all of our earliest realizations that we can't fly. My older brother had fed my sister popsicles to keep her from crying until Mom returned and authoritative action could be taken.

My mother had just gone back to full-time work, staying long into the evenings with her new training. She was trying to support our family after my father's business had folded and he suffered a complete breakdown. She was essentially a single mother now.

After being charged with fraud, my father's self-respect, self-esteem, and self-everything consequently began whirlpooling down the drain of life to devastating effect, eventually taking his sanity with it. Most evenings after my mother got in late from work, she filled her wine glass while she cooked us a beautiful dinner. With the illusion that what was prepared on the table was sufficient, my mother would retire into her own world of ghosts, the muttered warnings about marrying along with the sound of ice in the glass clinking in our ears.

"Remember, it is just as easy to love a rich man as a poor one," she liked to remind me as she reached over to gently tuck my hair behind my ear while I ate my dinner. Early on, then, I decided it would be best not to marry at all—or, if I happened to be stupid enough to somehow let it happen, to be sure to play my cards close to my chest.

The year before this picture was taken, my dad called during my sixth birthday party. We still lived in our grand house then, the one with hallways branching right and left, with the new master bedroom addition and the courtyard out back, over-branched by our beloved cherry tree, all bedazzled by birds. The children were downstairs playing games in the cool of the basement on the hot summer day. My mother beckoned me upstairs to pick up the phone, and so I reluctantly left behind my friends and the round of prizes my brother had been dispensing.

When my mother spoke these days, I listened for the restoration of her old voice—maybe it would return for my birthday? My mother used to always sing: it seemed she woke singing, cooked singing, drove singing, hosted birthday parties singing, dried us off from the bath singing. But now she rarely sang, and when she did, it wasn't the funny songs she used to giggle through with us, but only the sad ones sung along with the radio. She didn't even say our names the same way. It wasn't that happier voice beckoning me upstairs, not appearing even on my birthday. Instead, Mom just called out wearily again that it was my father on the phone. At this news, I shot up the carpeted steps, burning my knees exposed under my party dress as I scuttled on all fours. I had expected my father to return anytime that special day—surely he was running late only because of some surprise for me? I rounded the corner into the kitchen and greedily grabbed the phone, the receiver with the long cord swinging from the wall like a twisted beige vine. The excitement remained palpable. My father had called, and he was asking for me! I wrapped myself up in the cord, a coiled spring of birthday daughter delight.

The disappointment swallowed back bitterly when I heard he wouldn't make it home for my birthday.

"Stuck traveling, you know. I am sorry, my girl," Dad's voice sounded very far off indeed.

"Not even tonight? I can wait up for you. I know I can stay up late. I know I can! I won't get tired, I promise, and it's my birthday, so I know mom will let me!" I tried not to yell. Grandma said that was unbecoming in little girls. She told me that one could be *urgent* without yelling. I tried to be *urgent*, acceptably.

"No." He sounded tired. *Didn't he know it was my birthday? How could he sound tired?* "I can't be there, honey. You go enjoy your party, okay?"

How could he not be here? I gulped into the phone. I unwound my body and then began twisting the cord around and between my fingers, tying myself to his voice in some way.

He must have heard my silence, because he added unsteadily, "Mom is there, she will take care of it all. I'm sure the party is great fun."

I said nothing again.

"Look, what dress are you wearing, sweetheart?" he asked.

"My sunshine dress," I replied glumly, not feeling at all very sunshine-y. My sunshine dress was my favorite dress: bright yellow with small white polka dots and a real satin sash that tied up in a bow at my back, just like the girls in white dresses with blue satin sashes from the *Sound of Music*. Thanks to my mom, I always sang "My Favorite Things" when I put on this dress, although my sash was white and the dress, yellow. Perhaps I sang more brightly because it was yellow—and because my dad had given it to me as a gift when my sister was born two years ago. It fit more tightly each time I put it on, I noticed recently, but I was determined not to give it up, even if the sash went around my chest now and the hem really wasn't very lady-like, as my grandmother had remarked.

"Well, why don't you go outside right this minute and stand by that tall tree, you know, the one out front, and have mom take your picture in that dress? That way, as soon as I do get home, I will get to see you exactly as you look now."

"When will you be home?" I asked quietly.

"I don't know, honey," my dad replied just as quietly. "I have to put things right, and that takes some time."

What things? How much time? How right? I thought to myself. But before I could ask, my dad told me to give the phone back to my mom. I heavily passed the receiver to her, as if it weighed more than I could bear. She took it from me with an effort that appeared similar to my own. My heart felt just as heavy, and I became aware for the first time of how absence can be a presence of the weightiest kind. Patting my head, she sent me back downstairs. I blinked back tears on the descent. My friends' smiling, upturned faces met me as I rounded the stairs. Full of sugared gaiety, they sat barely containing themselves in a group playing duck duck goose. Forcing a smile, I took my place in the circle and joined in the game.

.··ılıllıı.

The drive to the hospital takes place in *kairos* time. The maneuvering of lanes, the pushing of buttons to emit a ticket, the hunt for a parking space, and the tight shimmying of our Cheerios-encrusted minivan into a spot: How do all such mundane acts become ones bathed in ultra-awareness when faced with our mortality, or even more joltingly, with the mortality of a loved one? The seventh birthday photograph made the drive wedged in the empty cup holder. I stuff it into my purse and sprint from the parking lot through the sliding doors into the ER. I finger the picture nervously as the admitting nurse takes my information and tells me to wait a moment while they locate my father's bed. Then she gestures for me to follow her right away.

Passing through the second set of swinging doors, I'm immediately swept up with a wave of ambulance arrivals flowing in from a serious car wreck. A mad frenzy of paramedics, doctors, and nurses intermingle in the corridors, which are already thickly lined with other patients waiting for help. Some are vomiting into bowls, some are pressing bandages to stop up bleeding wounds, and some are muttering to themselves and wandering about the waiting areas. Canada's "free" health care offers both a blessing and a curse: treatment is affordable if the wait doesn't kill you first.

By the time I see my father, my breath catches at just how old he suddenly appears. He lies completely still on a hospital bed in a slightly more private space, cordoned off from the fray by a thin curtain. His face looks very white, and even his hair seems to have silvered more completely—a reluctant prophet spat forth from a great whale. His hand feels cold in mine.

"You will need to step out while we complete the next set of tests," the doctor explains.

I nod and somehow manage to follow the meandering halls back to the doors that swing between my only current worlds—inside the ER, and outside. I now understand why so many hospitals paint a path in and out of the labyrinth of corridors from ERs: an ironic yellow brick road to and from pulled-back curtains, a golden thread by which to navigate the monsters.

Back in the waiting room of the large urban hospital, I take a seat between a homeless man muttering to himself and a very thin woman who is obviously high. With no cell signal in this part of the hospital, I find myself at a loss for something to do, so I take out the photo I brought along and study it more carefully. I raise the young me to my older eyes and see furtive excitement personified, a seemingly typical child waiting to exhale over a simple cake.

I look at the photo more deeply. A mother now myself, I can see my mother's race to the grocery store, the need (among oh so many needs) to make something special for a little someone special on so very little. I understand the selection of cake, its barrenness, in the paucity of time and money. And yet where did she find that candle? And what motherly flourish—a glorious, unabashedly slink of pink that flamed the little single-roomed antique cottage with such delight! Only my sister and I sit at the table. My brother, older by a decade, was at his summer job. My mother took the picture, which is why parts of our heads are clipped from the frame, as were all photos my mom took before she was diagnosed years later with having "only one good eye"—something we teased her about mercilessly with adolescent humor. "Oh dear," she would say sweetly or sarcastically in response (one could never quite tell which, with my mom). Sometimes, after a long drive together, she would announce, "I got shampoo in my one good eye this morning." To this day, whenever we look through family albums and see our guillotined figures, we know who took the picture.

The birthday celebration took place in the tiny dilapidated cottage along Lake Erie that my paternal grandmother received in exchange for dues owed to her by a client. This old cabin became the mainstay of my childhood, the only place amid a steady turnover of houses that remained a safe and stable place to go. My father's mother, a self-made businesswoman, immigrated to Canada from Poland as a young woman in an arranged marriage, only to find herself raising two boys on her own shortly after arriving in a new land. She achieved this while running a diner and a beauty salon, and eventually getting a realtor's license on the side. With her usual perfect foresight, earned by having survived the Great Depression era, I note in the birthday photo how she has spread out newspapers beneath our plates and cups as a cheap precaution against costly spills. I close my eyes and enter more fully into the memory: how the black newsprint mirrors itself on my hands whenever I forget and rest them on the table. Usually a fastidious child (often annoyingly so), I don't mind being sullied such today. The cartoon Pink Panther candle, with its head of flames, captivates my attention as I inhale deeply and prepare my wish. My father, as was almost always the case while I was growing up, is not in the picture. As a result, his head escaped being cropped—though, I came to learn later, not his heart.

I look up from the photo, blinking back into the current reality of the hospital waiting room. The homeless man beside me, who literally looks like Tom Hanks in *Cast Away*, leans in close to look at the photo too. I hold my breath for a myriad of reasons.

"Whoa," he says, I assume in response to my seventies-era dress and Dorothy Hamill hair in the photo. But then he points at the cake and gives my arm an admiring nudge. "Nice candle."

I smile but say nothing. I don't tell him that, in the time it takes to blow out a candle, the house full of singing and the opulent cherry tree and the party with friends were gone. So was being dressed in sunshine. So was the loving father. So were all the answers. My smile fades as I say nothing of the ghosts who sat at our dinner table and have raised their glasses ever since. Somehow, I suspect he might already understand.

I take one last long look at the photo before pocketing the memory away: a seemingly fatherless little girl turning seven, pursing my lips as if to kiss my wish into being, and then blowing. And, like a good little girl, I never told anyone my wish.

Chapter One

SAVED SEX

*Virtue and vice are not the same, even if
they undergo the same torment.*

St. Augustine

*A*t the hospital, a nurse came out
to find me in the waiting room.
She then ushered me into one of the little rooms tucked along the
hospital corridor leading away from the chaos of the ambulance entrance. Two signs decorated the door: the larger one read in bold
letters, "**Private Consultation**" while the smaller one just below it
stated in more demure script, "*Please knock before entering.*" The nurse
took a key and unlocked the door, revealing a small, dark room. I
looked into that darkness, so much starker against the bright lights
of the busy hospital hall. While I welcomed a reprieve from the kind
of bloody, groaning, and antiseptic commotion unique to a hospital
emergency wing, I hesitated at the threshold like Dante at the lip of
hell, with the words inscribed above: "Abandon all hope, ye who
enter here." Good news surely does not reach into overlooked spaces
such as these. I took a deep breath and stepped inside.

"Would you like some water?" the nurse asked with compassion in her voice. I declined. She reached over and clicked on the single small lamp beside the door.

"Please, make yourself comfortable." She patted my arm. "The doctor will be with you shortly."

I am always amazed at the infinite capacity of nurses for caring (I tell you, sit me next to the nurses and the drummers in heaven). She left, pulling the door shut softly behind her.

Insulated within this little room that seemed to scream uncannily quiet, I could now pace out my impatience. *Where was that doctor? What would the next test say?* I couldn't help but think of one of my dad's favorite short prayers: *Lord give me patience, but hurry up!* I decided to sit after all. I pulled up one of the two chairs separated by a small table holding a telephone and scratchpad with pen. Some previous visitor to this room, most likely also awaiting heartbreaking news on a loved one, had printed a single word on the page in capital letters, underlining it so severely that the imprint scored through several pages: *WHY?*

Sometimes the *whys* tumble all together so fast and furiously that I cannot pull all the threads apart. They sting like a million arrows—like the etymology for the word *sin*—somehow all missing the mark. The *whys* of why things happen and the *whys* of why they don't. The myriad of parallel lives that could have been all pointed to the life that should have been, underscoring all the more painfully what life was intended to be, but now (literally) falling short on this side of heaven.

I traced the line under the *WHY?* on the scratchpad with my finger. *Why now, when my father and I finally have such peace and unfettered love between us? Why now, when grandchildren gather about his knee and give him more joy than he had ever known over a lifetime of obstacles and isolation? Why now, when my father and I share our God and our faith and a deeper line of communication, vulnerability, and trust? Why now, after years of heartbreak, when it was finally so sweet?*

In the last few years since my husband and I and our young family returned to my hometown, we had shared our faith with my father and watched him open up to it and grow in it too. Deep reconciliation happened, which had been such an immense blessing. And then having a surprise baby we named for him, and seeing his joy at such naming: I knew I should be grateful for any healing on this side of heaven—and I was—but I was still greedy for more. Is this a bad thing? This insatiable longing? I used to feel guilty about it, but I've grown to appreciate it, to even embrace it as only more indicative of our homesickness for God and his great overflowing of goodness for which we yearn. "My grace is sufficient," Jesus tells us. On some days, I reply "Amen." On others, I say, "Oh really?" And on others still, I somehow hold both together. This was one of those amen-with-a-question-mark sort of days.

Our pastor once preached about how the Bible teaches us not so much to ask, "Why?" when bad things happen, but instead, "What now?" I thought about his words as I stood up but resisted the urge to pace. I wished to be receptive to this strange peace settling around me in this suddenly holy space. In that darkling room, the epic poet John Milton's closing words to his sonnet on becoming blind as a writer came to me: "They also serve who only stand and wait."

And then, in accordance with the sign, the knock came.

.ılılllııı.

Was it really all those years ago now when other knocks came? That day had been stormy too. The air hung limp with humidity and yet was electrified by the promise of lightning. Thunder rolled low across the ravine behind our house, where the Native American Archeology

Museum was reconstructing the original village from remnants secreted within the earth.

An awful tempest mashed the air,
The clouds were gaunt, and few;
A black, as of a spectre's cloak,
Hid heaven and earth from view.

It was my first birthday back home in Canada after beginning my studies at Oxford University and, incidentally, my first birthday as a Christian. I had spent the earlier part of the day celebrating with my mom and younger sister before they left for work. Now it was just the cat and me at home. We lay melted out on the back patio, me in the lawn chair and the cat underneath my shade, both of us too warm to do much else but listen to the distant thunder. I had a mountain of school reading to get to, but couldn't be bothered. Obviously, neither could my cat, as she gave a disgruntled sigh when I finally got up to refill my lemonade glass. I had just come in through the back patio door when I heard a knock at the front door. When I opened it, I was surprised to see my ex-fiancé standing there.

We had barely talked, let alone seen each other, since our breakup over Christmas. This was the first summer in years when we weren't an item. I froze in the doorway, caught in a swirl of thoughts and emotions. I barely managed a nod in return to his hello.

Simply put, we had broken up over God. I wanted to pursue a life of faith, and Ben wanted to pursue a life without it. He thought the two approaches were compatible and not a long-term concern; I saw them as distinct life views and didn't want to knowingly enter marriage on such uneven footing. In our breakup, we were amicable though mutually hurt. He had gone on to date someone else seriously—they were on the brink of moving in with each other but had decided to take a break, or so I heard from mutual friends.

In the meantime, I had enjoyed a season of growing closer to this God of my discovery. And, if I was honest, I had begun to realize my growing appreciation—and attraction—for a dear friend who had been the first to clearly and kindly not only articulate the gospel to me, but to model it as well.

My friends and I goofily referred to this man as "TDH," meaning "Tall, Dark, and Handsome." He was also an American studying at Oxford: smart, funny, and terribly sweet-hearted. Unaware of my growing feelings for him (I would rather die than let on), he had left England that summer for a job at a think tank in Washington, DC. I feared we'd never see each other again and tried to make peace with this reality, which, I congratulated myself, I had done quite nicely. I did this largely by concentrating on what irritated me about TDH: his steadfast obedience and love for God, which he somehow pulled off without being pious or phony (which initially had irritated me even more). And, oh yes, his darling obliviousness to how attractive other women found him, too, drawn to his gentility, which try as I might to discover otherwise, kept proving itself to be genuine. He occupied a category completely of its own: one I had hoped deep down inside existed, but dared not trusted to be so. No, his type didn't exist in this world, not among many of the men I knew, nor from the experiences of my girlfriends, nor in the news or media— and certainly not in academia, where a man who loved God might be considered an unenlightened, constrictive conservative at best or a neo-Neanderthal at worst. Heaven forbid a man should open a door for you or pull back a chair from the dinner table . . . now that my categories were jumbled and my expectations raised, well, there seemed no going back, or below.

But that was then, and this was now. Very *now*. Suddenly Jesus and faith and TDH and other men like him seemed very far away as I stood in that doorway looking at Ben's very real, gentle smile. Things had grown serious between Ben and me during our college years together because of our many points of common interest. We came from the same town and were both academics; we shared interests in music, food, travel, and hobbies. We respected each other. Ben was kind and easygoing, with a promising career ahead of him and a warm family. A real catch, as my mom liked to remind me. She still seemed convinced that our breakup was only temporary. Me leaving anyone for Jesus made her categorically nervous. And how could anyone outdo Ben? Successful, thoughtful, dependable Ben? For me now, however, something was missing for him, in him . . . just as it had been for and in me, too, and I longed for him to find and be found by it. I longed for him to have his life transformed by grace too.

And yet I stood in the doorway and said nothing.

Ben had liked to remind me that we don't need God to be good. I would reply that I definitely needed God to be good, and in fact I needed him to be the best there was, and is, and ever will be!

"Don't play syntax games with me," Ben would say, frowning. "You know what I mean. God isn't necessary for someone to act morally." It was like hanging out with Iris Murdoch-meets-Ernest Hemingway.

But I did need God for me to be good as much as I needed him to be exactly who he claimed to be. And even when I thought of all the "good" people I knew who didn't know God, something was missing there, too, as opposed to those whom I began to see had a living faith. The latter may make mistakes, like everyone else, but at least they had a frame of reference for how the human condition is a powerful paradox of humility and dignity. Without an understanding of sin, and particularly an acknowledgment of our own, and without the acceptance and extension of grace, how can anyone even approach being "good" past the conditional, fair weather, or even lucky? And for those who were truly trying to be good, for whom their characters spoke of someone dependable, kind, and true, wasn't this approaching God anyway, and shouldn't they just throw in the towel and believe, if they didn't already, given their affinity? I mean really, if you can't beat them, why not join them? For if God is for us, indeed, who is against us?

Ben would argue, "Look at all the atrocities done in the name of religion!"

To which I would reply, "Look at all the atrocities done in the lack of religion!"

And it would be a draw. But somehow not the kind I could take easily to the marriage altar.

Must we recognize the source, actually *see* it and claim it for God's, for it to be God's? Or is God actually at work in and through such good, more often and more anonymously than we tend to give him credit? After all, everything that sings of the love of Christ testifies to the love of Christ: the hug of a friend (regardless of religious affiliation), the beauty in an act of empathy, the splendor of a sunrise, the goosebumps created by even a rock-and-roll song? Why not tether similar strands together, or recognize the strains without for the music within? Where there is smoke, there is indeed fire.

Speaking of fire . . .

"Can I come in?" Ben gave me a long look.

Still unable to speak, I nodded, stepping aside. Something seemed off, something askew. There was a time when he would have swept in and kissed me on the cheek as he passed by before throwing himself haphazardly on my couch. But now a formality had settled in between us, vined its way around our words and actions, so that we stood in the hallway like acquaintances rather than people who had once planned a life together.

"Would you like something cold to drink?" I offered him, unsure of what to do.

"That'd be great," he said quickly, seeming equally uneasy. Having lost her main source of shade, my cat had followed me into the kitchen, wrapping herself around my leg. Ben and I stood at the counter and drank our lemonades in silence.

"I wondered if you'd like to go for a drive?" he finally said softly. "You know, for old times' sake?"

We always used to take a drive on my birthday, usually to the lake along some scenic route.

"Well . . ." I stiffened, drawing circles in the condensation on my empty, cold glass.

"Sorry," he shrugged, turning away. "Habit."

I didn't say anything.

"I should go." He walked toward the door.

"No, wait." I felt badly. I missed him. Or, I missed the idea of him. Or perhaps I missed the idea of me? Who was I, exactly? Home now with a new faith in an old life? In the world and not of it? How much easier it would be *not* to be a Christian! Not to be, well . . . *good*.

The inner chastising began too: Why, I reasoned, should I flinch at the idea of going for a simple ride with a man who only a few months ago I thought I was going to marry? It is my birthday after all—I had celebrated every birthday for the last several years in the exact same way with this exact same person. It made sense to take one last ride together too. I owed him that much, regardless of the tension between us. And what was this "tension," really? That Ben didn't believe in God, and I now did? Maybe he had a point: Was that really such a big difference after all? Ben was kind, funny, dear. He was no monster atheist—in fact, he was more loving than some who seemed to proclaim a love for Christ appeared to be. Ben made it very clear that he considered faith a crutch for the weak, that he didn't believe in anything or anyone but himself. I had felt that way, too, or at least close to it, but now I wasn't so sure anymore if not believing wasn't some kind of faith as well?

And besides all that, Ben owned a really cool vintage truck. *Oh, I am incorrigible*, I scolded myself. Here at home, I was involved with a man who had no faith in God, and at Oxford, I was drawn to a man who did. Was I unsettled by both of these men, or maybe—just maybe—was it God, whether through his (seeming) absence or his presence, that disturbed me most?

Ben looked at me uncertainly, awaiting my answer. Then he held out a hand, a gesture of peace. I took it in mine, moved by its familiar calloused feel from working the fields during his summer break. It was the first time we had touched in a very long time, this man who had been my college sweetheart. Tanned from his work on the farm, his hair had lightened almost to white blond. I wanted to smooth his wayward cowlick like I used to do, but forced myself not to move a muscle. He smelled like good earth and meadow air, I noticed as he stepped closer, slipping his other hand around my waist. *Those Amish romance novels sell at a clip for a reason*, I thought to myself. "Men who make do undo me," declares Joan Anderson. Indeed.

Why is it those infamous opening notes of Lynyrd Skynyrd's "Sweet Home Alabama" always seem to rise up in the back of your mind whenever you are about to kiss your ex from your hometown? And oh, for a moment as long as longing itself, how I longed to kiss him. Standing there wearing his familiar khakis and button-down shirt, he seemed so much more real than Jesus. How familiar it would be, reassuring: the tactile reality of someone who did love me, rather than the distant consideration of a God who might.

Who *might*?

But wait, *wait* . . .

I pulled back and grabbed his keys off the counter. "Let's go!" I called as I sprinted for the door, tossing the keys to him over my shoulder like salt in the devil's eye.

.ıılıllıı.

The sun sat low on the dashboard as we continued driving toward the lake. The old truck rattled and hummed along the country roads. By the time we pulled up at the little cottage from my youth, the air hung thick with cricket song. Once on the front porch, I ran my hands above the door, feeling for the hidden key on the hook. Not exactly the most original of hiding places, but then again, there was nothing worth stealing in the century-old place anyway.

The cottage consisted of essentially one large room, with two small bedrooms (if you could call them that) cordoned off from the main space by curtains, not doors. A tiny galley kitchen, with a two-burner stove and a sloping floor, ran the length of the back wall. When you opened the refrigerator door, you had to be careful to hold it steady or else it would slam against the cupboard with all the force of inclined gravity. You had to shut it tight, too, and double check, or else it would slowly creak back open and you'd return to your goods stored there at dismal room temperature with a puddle of water at your feet. Electricity had been put in years after the cottage was built, and so the exposed wiring unapologetically veined the walls. The tiny bathroom with running water had been an afterthought too. As a result, a compact shower, sink, and toilet sat haphazardly off the kitchen with a flimsy cardboard door propped open by a large stone from the beach that you scraped heavily along the floor to use as a doorstop or a lock, whichever was required.

We hastily unlatched a few windows to ward off the musty smell. Now that all the grandchildren were grown and many of them gone, my family rarely came here. Walking in brought a rush of memories, particularly of childhood birthdays past, as I was the only one besides my father with the midsummer birthday.

I didn't see the kiss coming. The room grew dim; the world seemed to recede away from us. A dark tide swirled around my ankles. Ben, who always did love Matthew Arnold, whispered the poet's closing lines from "Dover Beach" in my ear: "Ah, love, let us be true to one another . . ."

So unfair! How was I to withstand such effrontery? Poetic words undo me about as much as calloused hands from honest work: put them together, and . . . oh I would have been lost indeed had an Irish lilt or Scottish brogue come into the mix as well!

But Arnold's poem is forlorn, I found myself countering . . . a warning! Alas, the tide, velvet and warm, rose higher still, shaking my knees, dashing my hips . . . my eyes began to close. Oh my. It is a hard thing indeed to concentrate with another's lips at the pulse of your throat.

Wait, what does Jesus say about kissing your former fiancé?

But there seemed no time to think. All the time in the world for desire, but none at all to think. Time and desire became one, and thinking was the last of my concerns.

Ben took my hands and pulled me gently into the backroom with the old brass bed, the bed I had spent every summer in as a child through my teenage years. It still wore the same bedspread, white as a bride's dress, and quilted with rosebuds, now faded but pretty still. We lay down together, Ben's face so close I could see the tears glistening in his eyes. He brushed back my hair as he kissed me. Suddenly, the tide rushed my heart.

"Who will know?" he whispered into the gush of floodgates opening.

"Yes, who will know?" I echoed.

Who will know?

I sat up straight, almost toppling Ben off the bed.

I will know.

God will know.

Oh, that sounds so Gothic, I scolded myself. *So . . . heavy.* Just the words themselves seemed engraved in rock. Like someone had tossed me a stone tablet and I lay crushed underneath. How relevant could such a truth possibly be?

But ay, there's the rub! And indeed sometimes it rubs right up against you: the truth may not be convenient, but it is always relevant. It knows of no other way to be.

"Surely this breaks no commandment?" Ben said with such eerie resonance I jumped. He reached over and started rubbing my shoulders, easing me backward toward him.

I didn't say anything. We weren't married to other people, after all, and we obviously still cared for each other. We had a history, the perfect opportunity yawned before us . . . and indeed, who would know? I hesitated, though Ben did not seem to notice. Was it guilt? Was it shame? Was it fear? Lynyrd Skynyrd's lyrics rose up: *Lord, I'm coming home to you . . .*

No, it ran deeper than those self-judgmental and cultural knee jerks. Somehow, the answer felt, well, more *intimate.* More intimate, even, then what was happening all around me and to me. Something so intimate as to come deep from within, from something stronger and surer than bodily fluids or even wandering thoughts.

You shall have no other Gods before me.

The words flashed before me in my absence of thought like the swing of a double-edged sword. And then they were gone.

I didn't yet know much Scripture by heart; in fact, with an older brother as a disc jockey I knew way more rock lyrics than holy verses. I was new to this faith, a latecomer to the Bible, unchurched and still streaming cynicism behind me at times. But these words, this first commandment, rose up before me for some crazy reason at the most inopportune time. I have since learned that Scripture has a way of doing that. Beware. It makes no ordinary sense. It reads like no pedestrian prose, no mundane poetry. It is, indeed, as Dietrich Bonhoeffer claims, in a class all its own. Holy? I used to wonder at the adjective that appeared in front of the simple title on my Bible. *Holy!* Then I realized that they should put an exclamation mark after it. The echo left my body taut, as though I was straining to hear something I could not quite hear. Unaware, Ben kept on kissing my throat, my collarbone, his hands moving deftly down the buttons of my summer blouse.

All of the sudden, there came a knock at the door. Quietly at first. I wasn't even certain if I had heard it. I craned my neck further from the bed, which Ben mistook for ecstasy and so returned to kissing it again more fervently.

That didn't help. I closed my eyes. Surely I was mistaken?

No, there it was again. *Bang. Bang. Bang.*

My eyes shot wide open. I peered over Ben's shoulder, as though sharpening my focus would help me hear better.

"Ben," I whispered. "Stop. Someone's at the door."

"That's crazy," he replied in a muffled voice between kisses. "This place is in the middle of nowhere. No one even knows we're here." He went back to determinedly wrestling with an equally determinedly stuck button.

The knock came again, louder still. This time we both jumped at the sound. There was no denying it; even Ben paused and raised his head.

"The place is virtually abandoned, for Christ's sake!" he said angrily, standing up and tucking his shirt into his pants. I, too, virtually abandoned, lay half-dressed and half dazed on the bed. His outburst grated me like it hadn't before.

"You shouldn't take the Lord's name in vain," I half-joked at him. Everything seemed at halves.

Ben tossed me a fed-up look.

"That's a commandment, you know," I added lamely. I had commandments on the brain now too.

The knocking reverberated even more loudly this time: *BANG! BANG! BANG!* Jumping up, Ben and I stared at each other. "It's like the knocking at the gate of *Macbeth*!" I cried, filled with mock doom.

"What?" whispered Ben, looking at me like I had lost my mind. He was an economist, I reminded myself, not an English major. I had been living among literary geeks who tend to speak a language of allusion, to advantage and disadvantage.

"You better go answer it," Ben prodded me. "It's your cottage, you know."

"It's not *my* cottage," I hissed. "It's technically my grandmother's."

Ben stared at me. I realized what I just said made what we were just doing even worse.

Now we all did what we could do.

"What if it's a crazy derelict?" I cried again. The only other time someone uninvited knocked on this door was years ago when I was up late playing cards with my sister. He proved to be a drunk trying to find his way home from the beachside pub.

"I'll be right behind you," Ben insisted.

So much for chivalry, I thought to myself as I haphazardly fastened my buttons and threw my hair back in a ponytail. The inner tide ebbed as I straightened my clothes.

"Carolyn, come on, maybe one of our friends figured out we came here for your birthday? I can't let them see me here. They'll tell Rebecca. I better stay back until we know who it is."

Now it was my turn to stare at him, every drop of attraction evaporating fast.

Does your conscience bother you? Tell the truth.

"I thought you said you two were taking a break?" I finally managed to croak. The tide was clearly out now: no sign of it, land ho!

"We're still sleeping together, whenever she comes home from college, we're just not, well, *serious . . .*" he paused.

"Sex seems pretty serious to me," I replied flatly. Anger tendrilled up between us.

"Oh, you . . . *Christians!*" he spat the word at me. "Making such mountains out of every molehill."

I forced myself not to look at the undone zipper of his pants with a cynical air. Irritated beyond belief, or perhaps irritated back into it now, I bolstered myself, inwardly preparing for what all English majors will recognize as *the* Jane Eyre speech.

I adored Jane Eyre's famous speech to Rochester, the one she gives when he wants her to be his mistress but she stands firm in her God-given dignity. No regular pre-suffrage lady's speech. No swooning woman there. Three hurrahs for Jane!

Why then was I, so modern and well, so *Christian,* now so wobbly-kneed and foggy-headed? Alas, however, try as I might, I couldn't get my footing. The familiarity, the still being wanted, the, well, *feeling . . .* it all seemed so unfair! If I couldn't muster Jesus, it seemed, at least I could muster Jane.

But just before the fury crackling between us blew into full flame, Ben closed his eyes. In spite of everything, I felt my heart twist. The earthquake, the fire, and then . . . the small, still voice.

"I'm sorry," Ben said gently. "I meant," he stammered, "Rebecca and I aren't serious . . . like you and I were . . . well, before . . ." he put his hands to his face and said in a muffled voice, "before God got in the way."

I had to admit, he had a point. For Christ's sake, literally, and all of ours, I felt my eyes tear up too. Why is life so messy?

Ben rubbed his eyes. Suddenly I realized how tired he looked. I felt tired too.

"I'm just, oh I don't know, Caro . . . confused. I don't know what I feel anymore." Ben spoke so guilelessly, I didn't know whether to slap him or hug him. I had proven I couldn't yet be trusted hugging him, and I figured that slapping him didn't convincingly represent the faith I wanted to model to him, which, I had to admit, I hadn't done very well at so far. So instead, I just sat down heavily on the edge of the bed, tracing with my finger the circlet of roses along the wedding dress quilt.

By grace go each of us. By small circles of grace, over and over again.

"I'm sorry too," I replied. I had the feeling we were both apologizing for different things, but trusted the intersection had us covered.

Unsure now what to do with his hands, Ben put them in his pockets. He gave me a weak smile and said, "I'll get the door."

"I've got it," I said, smiling back and getting up. "You stay here. I'll call out if he's armed and dangerous. There's a good-sized cast iron pan in the kitchen if we need it."

The knocking had continuously grown stronger, rattling the old screen door against the flimsy inner wooden one. I feared the antique cottage would come down if I didn't get to it soon.

When I opened the door, sure enough, a crazy-looking derelict met my gaze through the locked screen door. There stood an unkempt man with tousled hair sticking out every which way from under a golf hat and wearing a full-length very wrinkled beige raincoat, although it was sweltering outside. He held a large box in front of him. He had been banging against the door with his foot. I noticed his boots didn't match.

It was my father.

"What took you so long?" he gruffed a greeting to me. He didn't wait for an explanation.

"This is heavy. Let me in."

I shook off my stunned disbelief and unlatched the screen door, opening it wide so I could help maneuver the box from his hands and set it down on the indoor woven rug. It was indeed heavy.

"What is in here, Dad?" I asked. "A body?"

My father shot me an unsure look. A little unsure myself, given my dad's colorful history, I tried a small laugh.

"You'll see soon enough," my dad smiled shyly at me, like a young boy.

I noticed from the corner of my eye that Ben remained partially hidden behind the little curtain to the bedroom, in my line of vision but not my father's. I could tell he was unsure of the terrain, too, and hesitating as to whether to make his presence known or not. I mouthed at him to stay put. My dad could be mentally confused in many ways, but I knew he could do life math: one look at my former boyfriend and me here together all alone in an isolated location on a late summer afternoon, and he'd be able to add things up pretty fast. After all, he was my father—fathers, even intermittent ones, still tend to own such uncanny calculation when it comes to their daughters. Moreover, my dad, technically, was at times what you might genteelly call "unstable." All this made for a particularly loaded combination when it came to finding daughters alone with suitors. Through the crack in the curtain, poor Ben looked as surprised—and alarmed—as I felt.

"How did you know I was here?" I stuttered accusingly at my dad. I still couldn't believe he was standing in front of me. At that time in my life, I rarely saw my father; his comings and goings were random indeed. There was never any rhyme or reason to his visits, and if he did visit, it was usually late at night at the home I shared with my mom and younger sister or sometimes at a special event at school, where he appeared without warning and embarrassed us. How I envied the other kids with fathers who showed up in normal cars, with normal clothes, and who held normal conversations! Fathers who didn't rant and rave, or bring along chums from the shelter who slurred their words. Fathers who didn't wear Salvation Army motleys and drive a van rusted through the floorboards with a caged dog barking nonstop in the back. I never understood how my friends could roll their eyes and call their dads "embarrassing" when they ate their birthday dinners together in comfortable restaurants, or joked around after their fathers dropped them off at the school dance with the announcement of when they would be back to pick them up. In the handful of times I agreed to meet my father at a restaurant for some special occasion, it never ended well. A waiter would be insulted, or a table overturned, or a bill left for a struggling teenager daughter to pay after a fit of paranoia caused her father to flee. An ocean of difference rolls between mere embarrassment and humiliation, and I often found myself floundering in a riptide when it came to my father's unpredictable moods. I ached for someone to merely "embarrass" me by calling out he would be back for me at the end of the dance. In more ways than one, it seemed I had to make my way to and from everywhere alone, and usually in the dark.

As a general rule, my father didn't remember birthdays, and holidays weren't on his radar. Christmas was to be avoided in particular as it was a season that pained him ever since his own drunken father had beaten his mother to a pulp and left his young sons on Christmas Eve. I had birthdays pass without receiving so much as a card, but then some years an extravagant gift would come when I least expected it: a black Raleigh bike when I was ten; a fistful of lira just before I went to study art in Italy when I turned seventeen. And now this: my own bodyweight in a nondescript brown box. What could it be? And how did he know to find me here, of all places? Considering almost two decades of coming to this little cottage, I only owned a small handful of memories of him ever joining us here, but that was long before The Divorce. The discomfort between us only grew worse after his breakdown by the chasm caused by mental illness.

"Well, go ahead," he urged me, hesitantly radiant. "Open it!"

Typical of my dad, I thought at the time, the box was not only taped shut, it was taped all over. It looked like a square ball of transparent yarn. It took me some time just to saw through the sticky bondage with a butter knife from the small remnant of kitchen utensils. Later, I realized he was probably terrified of any of its contents getting ruined. But at the time, I just thought it was plain crazy. Perhaps growing in grace helps us withhold judgment so as to see the layers of precious within the precious. Nacred, we are, in such insights; like a pearl beyond price, the kingdom within sheens.

A distinct smell met me as soon as I opened the box. I shuddered.

And then I saw it . . .

Or, I should say, *them* . . .

Old books! That matchless scent of old books wafted over me . . . a beloved smell, so familiar and comforting. The smell of wisdom, of minds in endless conversation. The smell of civility and imagination and information and insight. The fragrance of *humanitas*, the scent of what it means to be truly humane.

Goosebumps of the best kind ran up my arms and down my legs as I kneeled down and gently pulled each book from its nestling in straw. With every extraction, I gasped in awe. Book after book emerged, each a rare one. By the time I emptied the box, I could barely breathe. Fanned out around me were a dozen books bound in leather or with ancient marbled cover, some with gilded spines and pages, others with embossed titles or bright illustrations. All were collectors' editions, each representative of the eighteenth and nineteenth centuries, the literary period I was studying.

Oh wait! The bounty proved a baker's dozen, however, for out of his inner coat pocket my father pulled one more. *Jane Eyre*! I clasped it to my chest like a long lost friend.

"I couldn't get that last one to fit in the box," my father admitted.

I sat back on my heels, shellshocked by such generosity and unsure of which one to revisit first. My father chuckled at my obvious glee.

"How did you know?" I stammered, letting my hands run over the beloved friends, afraid that if I left contact with them, they might vanish. That my dad might vanish with them.

"I have my ways," my father shrugged. He often used this phrase when we asked where he came up with an unexpected provision, like the old car with its back doors permanently locked for my sister when she began college, or the hermit crabs he produced complete with an aquarium when we wanted a pet, or the beautiful hand towels marked "funeral home" when we needed dorm supplies. We learned not to ask any more questions when he used this phrase. My father didn't specialize so much in child support as he did in surprise support. This birthday, he looked particularly delighted at my delight.

And delighted I was—all alight I was! Shelley, Byron, Keats, Longfellow, Wordsworth, Blake, Tennyson . . . Coleridge, too, I realized with a swallow. So many dear old friends sitting resplendently expectant in front of me. I was amazed my father even knew which authors I was reading. With patient impatience, I previously had tried explaining to him several times just what I was studying while away at school. He always seemed distracted, patiently impatient himself.

I now realized he had been paying attention and had done a little research. Uneducated himself, he felt intimidated by schooling, although he was impressively self-taught in many areas prior to his dissolution. A new appreciation for his resourcefulness and for such sheer generosity washed over me. Perhaps he was just as uncomfortable by our discomfort as I?

"How did you know I was here, Dad?" I stood up to hug him. He moved away instinctively at first. My father was not a big hugger. I stepped in closer and kissed his cheek. He blushed.

"What do you mean, honey?" he stepped further back, shyly.

The old panic in me began to rise, with the usual drag of suspicious fear whenever my father began to not make sense. This might prove tricky territory to navigate.

How could he ask that? I thought to myself. *I mean, isn't it obvious? He treks out here to a small lakeside port where he hasn't seen us since we were children—and even then, memories of him at birthdays are few and very far between. I have barely seen him since returning from school, even in my own home! And I certainly didn't tell him about any plans to come here today of all days—I myself didn't even anticipate coming here until just this afternoon. No one knows we're here—literally not a single soul. Why is he here? How is he here?*

My father stood fiddling with his hat in his hands, seemingly oblivious to my question. Again I asked him, clearly and carefully, how he found me here?

In reply, my father produced from his trench coat pocket a creased photo of me at the little cottage celebrating my birthday. It was my seventh birthday, as I can tell by the Pink Panther candle on the birthday cake.

"I've always carried it, honey." He reached out to stroke my hair. "I've always been with you on your birthday."

Instinctively I wanted to dodge his preening, and started opening my mouth in the habit of protest: *What? You were never there! You have never been there!* I wanted to argue with him, to set the record straight. Dissention can become habit too; the default of comfortable discomfort.

But then I looked at the books circled around my feet. Standing at the center of a gift of words, something gave me pause, so I stopped my own words as gift in response—always a good move when in doubt, or even better as I am learning, when in faith.

I thought about the wider way in which my father may have meant this statement. Being a Christian was slowly opening up to me how to receive grace, and how to give it—how, indeed, to live by it. How circles of it ripple out whenever we toss it out and reel it in. *Real* it in and the truth will set you free. "I will make you fishers of men," Jesus calls to his followers. By land or sea, grace goggles do indeed allow us to see into the depths—even the murkiest ones—a little better. I realized I had never thought this way about my father before. There he stood, saggy golf hat literally in hand, a little nervous perhaps, about how his now-gone-away-and-educated daughter might receive him and receive his gift. There we stood together, surprised too by our mutual delight—a little afraid it might crack or give way, but trusting it still. Three cords indeed are not easily broken. Him, and me, and Christ makes three.

"I believed I would find you here," he finally said, simply.

Ever since my father's nervous breakdown, his memories would conflate; he often forgot my birthday or felt uncomfortable about coming by during festivities. Yet this year he remembered and, for some reason, drove out to the cottage in his battered old blue van believing he would find me there. And he did. Faith proves a powerful GPS indeed.

Except for his incessant knocking, or perhaps I should say, kicking, at the cottage door that day, my father was remarkably gentle his entire visit. No outbursts, no demands. No complaints or raging against someone for some injustice, imagined or otherwise. And I did a pretty good job, if I do say so myself, of not picking any fights, or judging, or finding fault. Not because of me but because of Christ in me. Because Jesus' example spoke to me of being available and loving. And because, healed in him, and continuing on this side of heaven to heal in him, he had bid me go in peace.

Around that gifting of books, my father and I sat together and passed the peace between us while Ben remained cloistered in the bedroom. I believe he didn't dare breathe. I don't know what kept him the most still—fear of my father or fear of The Peace. For if Ben had emerged and joined us, he might have been forced to join such peace, and a forced peace is no peace at all.

I offered to return the photograph but my dad had me keep it. So I slipped it into one of the volumes, the collection of Victorian poets. I spied so many beloved names in the table of contents, and then my eyes fell on Christina Rossetti, whose very name itself sounds like poetry. Given the occasion, I opened the book up to Rossetti's poem, "A Birthday," and read it aloud to my dad:

> My heart is like a singing bird
> Whose nest is in a water'd shoot;
> My heart is like an apple-tree
> Whose boughs are bent with thick-set fruit;
> My heart is like a rainbow shell
> That paddles in a halcyon sea;
> My heart is gladder than all these
> Because my love is come to me.
>
> Raise me a dais of silk and down;
> Hang it with vair and purple dyes;
> Carve it in doves and pomegranates,

And peacocks with a hundred eyes;
Work it in gold and silver grapes,
    In leaves and silver fleurs-de-lys;
Because the birthday of my life
    Is come, my love is come to me.

"What does *that* mean?" my dad asked with joking seriousness.

In typical annoying literature student fashion, I took a deep breath, preparing myself to explain how Rossetti frequently refers to the second coming of Christ as the ultimate "birthday" in her work, and how this symbolizes the new kingdom replacing the old earth, an idea that is mirrored in the spiritual rebirth of the individual as well (hence, being made a "new creation" in Christ) . . . and how . . . but I stopped.

"She's happy because of the rebirth that love brings," I said instead.

"Oh," my dad replied. "And the love that rebirth brings too?"

"Yes, true," I happily agreed, surprised. I loved this rebirthing myself. I had never really "talked" literature with my dad before. I took his hand but only held it briefly. He often got uncomfortable when touched, and pulled away.

"She seems happy she was born, this poet?" he asked solemnly, sitting on his hands now.

"Yes, and reborn, I would say." Instead of being hurt at his pulling away, as I always had been, I decided to meet him where he was at, just as Jesus meets all of us, just as he met and meets me, often at our deepest hurt and at our sharpest pulling away. Sitting there with my dad, I handed our handlessness to God.

"It sure is pretty, honey." He smiled.

"Yeah," I agreed. "It sure is."

We sat together quietly for some time. Eventually my dad broke the silence.

"Who is the love of your life?" he asked with a sweet simplicity that took me by surprise—so many surprises—truly a surprise birthday party that day!

I looked at him. Was this a trick question? The old panic rose up again. He will expect me to say it is him, in his fiery Lear-like fashion. I found myself coiling tight inside. My own hands folded protectively across my chest.

And it *is* a trick question, but not in the usual sleight of hand amid our fallen emotions, scars, and hurts. Rather, it is a revelatory question: one that anchors in hope as it lifts you up. One that lays you open as the truth rushes in—a fearsome truth that fills all the voids and overflows our understanding, so that we may "have life, and have it to the full." I took a breath and prepared myself for sharing such a choosing: for speaking the name that ultimately divides. Or unites.

"God," I finally replied.

And I meant it. The clarity of my own voice surprising (again) even me.

"Now it is God, Dad."

I waited for his hurt look, for his voice to change and thunder, for his demand that I love him first. I had even started at the force of my assertion. It was as though scales fell from my eyes and suddenly I felt my heart hurt at all I had almost given away, a sordid boon.

My dad turned to me and said with a gentle earnestness, "Good girl."

I slowly let out my breath. Is he being facetious? Condescending? Is it the crazy part of him talking? Or—perhaps, just perhaps—is it his truth meeting mine? There was a time when the feminist in me would have gone on the attack. But since becoming a Christian, I had been learning to wait, to listen for the sound behind the words, for the multiple ways of reading them in God's script for me and for all of us. Bane or blessing? Like the wrestling Jacob, I grasped at the blessing and refused to let go.

Is there not, at the heart of every wish, a desire to be loved unconditionally? A twisting, a turning, in some way, to be blessed? When we purse our lips to blow out our birthday candles, someone has already breathed us into being. The same spirit passes through all bodies, across all geographies, into all time and space. This is the overt truth secreted within each of us: our birthright, our death rite, and our being made right again in the rich grace of being redeemed rather than revoked, removed or replaced.

Yes. Good, girl.

My father touched my cheek gently before reaching for the door. I moved toward him, so that my cheek met his hand.

"Give Ben my regards." He looked directly into my eyes, his own eyes dancing.

I started at Ben's name. Before I could stop myself, my head swung in the direction of the little bedroom. I could barely make out Ben's shadow behind the curtain as the last of the day's light faded. In the shared treat of my father's gift, I had actually forgotten he was there. What was worse, I had almost forgotten my dad didn't know he was there!

Or did he? For at that same moment I looked down at my blouse and was mortified to see that the buttons were done up at odds. I felt my face go hot.

Poised in the doorway, my dad nodded toward the side drive. "Nice truck."

I breathed a sigh of partial relief. Hopefully it was only the old Ford that gave it away. Regardless, the opportune knock, I had to admit, seemed a *Coitus Interruptus de Spiritu Sancto*. For then my dad asked rather loudly, it seemed, given I was still right in front of him: "How is that tall American fellow you mentioned? You know, the one you talked about sharing God with you?"

I felt my face grow even hotter. My dad winked. It would seem he listened more than I gave him credit for. *Honor thy father and thy mother.* I was slowly but surely learning that these commandments made more sense than I gave them credit for, as well.

"Give your mother my love, will you?" my dad said with his usual refrain. "I never stopped loving her you know."

And with that, he stepped outside and off the rickety porch with an easy athleticism that displayed itself at times in spite of his aging frame. I closed the screen door, and then, for good measure, also the old wooden door behind him. Weighed by the realization of my close call, I sunk down into the worn floral-patterned armchair.

"Is it safe to come out?" Ben asked at the click of the lock, emerging from the curtain like the assistant to a magician whose trick has just been foiled.

Safe?

Out of the box, I wondered what Jane would have had to say about that.

Chapter Two

THE SINGULAR LIFE

*The soul, then, lives by God when it lives well, for it cannot
live well unless by God working in it what is good.*

St. Augustine

Just the summer before, I had been preparing to leave my hometown and all I had ever known to study at Oxford University in England. My life, so it seemed to me, was all mapped out: I would complete the two-year master's program at Oxford and then return to do my doctorate in Canada, most likely Montreal, where I could easily take the train to visit my family and be close to Ben's place of graduate studies. Ben and I would marry, I would become a professor of literature, and we may or may not have children. We hadn't really given that any thought—we were much too preoccupied with our studies and career plans. The future was all tied up with a nice bow.

Why, then, did I feel like the ribbon was unraveling shortly after arriving in England? And what gift overflowed from the box in which it refused to be contained?

Part way through my undergraduate degree, my mother and I were able to pool together enough funds to finally purchase our own home—

it was nothing fancy, but it was in a better neighborhood than our previous place in the subsidized housing district. The duplex was closer to the university so my mom and I could commute together more easily: she as a secretary for the provost's office, and me to my classes.

One of our neighbors was an elderly, devout man who had taught theology and was busily committed to providing pastoral care to those in need at his church. It was well known in the neighborhood that he had been single his entire life but eventually got married at an older age to a woman who was his match in years but not in health. He knew she was dying when they married. Living in such proximity, I saw him almost daily, usually when he went outside to sweep his koi pond of leaves. He always smiled at me. Not once did I hear an unkind word from him. Not once, regardless of how pressed he must have been with the intricate care of his wife, did he seem rushed in his conversations with me. He gave me his full attention. He looked me in the eye. He remembered birthdays, and noticed when we were sick or had been away, often offering to help get our mail or do some yard tasks. Even at the time, such gentle grandfatherly attentions were not lost on my sister, mother, and me.

I asked him once how he could manage to be so kind, attentive, and patient when he . . . I didn't know how to say it . . . *How do you put into the words what I had witnessed: the contorted body of his wife, condemned to die a drawn-out death? . . .* so instead I stammered a paltry query: "How are you doing? I mean, how do you seem so peaceful when you have so much . . . going on?"

He gave me a soft smile—sad and sweet at the same time.

"You don't live with me, Miss Drake," he said. He often addressed me genteelly by my maiden name.

I laughed at what I took for a joke. I wasn't surprised, however, at his humility.

He looked me straight in the eye with his usual attentiveness. He wasn't joking, though he seemed joyful, somehow.

"Only one being truly lives with us," he said.

"You mean your spouse?" I assumed with adolescent confidence. Though inwardly I wondered, because I knew his wife was now bed-ridden and unresponsive.

"I guess you could say that." He smiled in his gentle way.

One beatific June afternoon, this kindly man called from his porch to catch me as I was leaving in my regalia for my graduation ceremony. His wife had died only a few weeks before, and yet he had a gradu-ation gift ready for me. As he passed me the card, he explained that the poem tucked inside had been attributed to Sir Francis Drake, the sixteenth-century explorer. He said he thought I might enjoy the words of someone with the same surname from so long ago, espe-cially as I now prepared to set out on my own grand adventure across the sea, leaving for my graduate studies in England at the end of the summer. At the time, I thought I would be studying literature, but I ended up learning so much more—I set out to do scholarly work on stories only to discover the greatest Story and our very real place within it. But at the brink of such an adventure, I had, as of yet, no inkling. Here is the Drake poem:

Disturb us, Lord, when
We are too pleased with ourselves,
When our dreams have come true
Because we dreamed too little,
When we arrived safely
Because we sailed too close to the shore.

Disturb us, Lord, when
With the abundance of things we possess

We have lost our thirst
For the waters of life;
Having fallen in love with life,
We have ceased to dream of eternity
And in our efforts to build a new earth,
We have allowed our vision
of the new Heaven to dim.

Disturb us, Lord, to dare more boldly,
To venture on wilder seas
Where storms will show your mastery;
Where losing sight of land,
We shall find the stars.

We ask You to push back
The horizons of our hopes;
And to push back the future
In strength, courage, hope, and love.
This we ask in the name of our Captain,
Who is Jesus Christ.

We stood there in the sunshine and birdsong, our hands joined by the passing of a piece of paper. So much is changed, always changed, changed always, by a single missive.

It would be much later when I actually read the poem—I mean, *really* read it. At the time, I simply took the card and tucked the gift under my arm and thanked him. Then I asked him hesitantly how he was feeling since the funeral.

"Sad. I miss her terribly. But relieved, too, if I'm honest. Carolyn, she trusted her Savior, and I need to trust too. When I think of our mutual hope, and the promise of heaven, I am joyful." He teared up but smiled.

A bit uncertain, I shifted my weight uncomfortably. Silence settled between us. My neighbor seemed at peace with the peace, but not me. No, never could I imagine at that time being at peace with such peace. A short time later, when I read G. K. Chesterton's fascinating novel *The Man Who Was Thursday*, I would resonate with its "trial" scene, in which the Secretary asks the leader named Sunday, "Who and what are you?" and Sunday answers, "I am the Sabbath. I am the peace of God." This enrages the Secretary, who most of us fist-shakers can identify with, for he replies:

> "I know what you mean," he cried, "and it is exactly that that I cannot forgive you. I know you are contentment, optimism, what do they call the thing, an ultimate reconciliation. Well, I am not reconciled. If you were the man in the dark room, why were you also Sunday, an office to the sunlight? If you were from the first our father and our friend, why were you also our greatest enemy? We wept, we fled in terror; the iron entered into our souls—and you are the peace of God! Oh, I can forgive God His anger, though it destroyed nations; but I cannot forgive Him His peace."

But at the moment on my neighbor's front porch, I merely blurted out, "I don't know how you did it. I mean, how could you marry her, knowing what was coming? And then watching her suffer . . . being there for her every need? How you went through it all? And then loving a God who would allow it!"

He said nothing.

"I mean," I insisted, again with all the honesty but obtuseness for propriety of my age, "how you took care of her, and must have felt so helpless! And then, well, losing someone you love like that—slowly and painfully, right before your very eyes. . . . How did you manage?

How can you . . ." I trailed off, preventing myself from asking how he could believe in this God he celebrated with the lighting of candles in his window every Sabbath. How could he, in a house full of impending death, darkened now in mourning, still practice this belief? How could he study and minister in death, and still *believe*? I kept grasping through my own tangled disbelief, feeling myself contorting painfully in the process, until I finally blurted out: "What did you do at the very end?"

He gave me a clear look of compassion tinged with sadness. Then he leaned in and kissed me gently on the cheek.

I fell silent, despite feeling the rising up yet again of that knee-jerk reaction toward unfairness, though at whom I could not name. It was the persistent assumption of a *whom* that struck me even then, however, and some strange understanding at the unspeakability of such a name. Something in me did not want to stay the same, either—but how to change? Could I change?

The kiss hummed on my cheek.

A car horn tolled, bringing me back to my sole self. I turned to go. I had experienced significant loss through those still living, yet not much loss by death, though I often wondered if that might be easier in comparison. I remained eager to get back to my friends waiting to celebrate graduation with all the gusto of the young who remain convinced such a passage secures everything that matters. The impatient honking from my driveway only underscored my conviction.

I climbed into my friend's waiting car and tossed the small, simply wrapped package on the dashboard. I ripped open the card and gave its contents and the poem a cursory glance as the radio blared loud and jokes filled the air along with laughter and plans for celebration. Forgotten in the flurry of living out dreams, I returned to read the words later, and later still, but there was always something else beckoning to be done—too many distractions for a truly meditative reading. The words were planted, but died, or so I thought. As I prepared that summer to move across the sea to begin my studies in the fall at Oxford University, I put it away among other books and papers.

.ıllıllıı.

A few months later I was home for Christmas, wavering between saying no to God and perhaps, just perhaps, saying yes. So much change had been happening in my heart in this relatively short span, and yet the change had been brewing for a long time coming. I sat in my old bedroom, the master that my mom had made sure I got to use as my own since it had a small walk-in closet that doubled as a study.

A pile of papers and packages teetered on the corner of my desk. My mom had been faithfully collecting my mail and arranging my desk while I was gone, and so I sat down and began sorting through the stack. At the very bottom, I came across the bubble envelope addressed to me from my elderly neighbor, the one I had tossed aside after opening the card, forgotten and overlooked. Curious now, I tore open the seal.

Inside was a copy of *The Brothers Karamazov*, the last novel published in 1880 by the Russian writer Fyodor Dostoyevsky. A bookmark had been placed inside its most famous chapter titled "The Grand Inquisitor," which addresses the problem of suffering and free will in a conversation between two brothers: the younger, Alyosha, a man of faith, and the elder, Ivan, an atheist. Ivan narrates to Alyosha a poetic account of how a leader from the Spanish Inquisition would have encountered Jesus, now returned to earth. In the imagined scene, the Inquisitor rejects Jesus and has him put in prison. In one of the most significant questions in the history of literature, the Grand Inquisitor stands before Jesus and asks: "Why have You come to disturb us?"

At the end of all the arguments, Jesus silently steps forward and kisses the old man. This stuns the Inquisitor, who releases Jesus with the admonition that he must never return. After Ivan finishes his story, Alyosha goes to him and kisses him gently, with an emotion beyond words. The usually skeptical Ivan cannot help the delight he takes in his brother's response to the poem with such a spontaneously meaningful gesture from it. The brothers then part ways.

Why have you come to disturb us? Even after years and years of teaching literature, this is one of the questions from a literary masterpiece that most haunts me. It rears up, inserting itself into my own life, and never failing to jolt me into the reminder of just what power—what unrivalled effect—the name of Jesus owns. The name is unlike any other name; its ability to disturb is unlike any other presence in the room.

In my own life, the question glints a double-edged sword of personal revelation. I had come home that Christmas on the cusp of a decision, at the threshold of two very different lives. I knew that accepting Jesus into my life would change everything, and though I wouldn't ever admit it, and didn't want to admit it, I was terrified. I felt like I was living out one of those "choose your own ending" storybooks—the kind that you read as a child where if you choose one page, you arrive at one ending, and if you choose another page, you reach a different fate. I could remain with everything that was familiar: my country, my family, my friends, my fiancé, an offered academic position at my alma mater, my way of being—my life that was full and exciting and interesting and yet . . . somehow, somewhere . . . well, *wanting*. Always wanting, in both senses of the word.

Or . . .

I could choose a different ending, a story without end, where my want had purpose, where my longing *and* my lack brought me to God, not away from him. Where so much meaning gleamed, I couldn't even look at it all head on, let alone take it all in. Where just to breathe is to praise, if we so will.

From my persistently fallen point of view, loving Christ can seem more of an interruption in what really "matters" than the reason for my existence. I sink into the soft pillow of complacency, which differs from the contentment that the apostle Paul speaks of having found in God, and which, interestingly, he writes of while in chains. If I am spurred to action, it is because I have swallowed the cultural placebo that somehow if I achieve "enough" I will have it all. This would be fine, would even be a soft-rolling truth to live by, a sort of permissible expectation, if it were not for Jesus' teachings and how we are called to live—and love—them out, even when we are not in the mood. As Augustine reminds us, "He who resolves to love God, and to love his neighbor as himself, not according to man but according to God, is on account of this love said to be of a good will; and this is in Scripture more commonly called charity, but it is also, even in the same books, called love."

I usually end up striving for some sort of ever-elusive equilibrium that seems to be the answer to it all. Just the fact that I seem to sense the existence of such a possible bar of satisfaction appears proof enough of a prelapsarian haunting of intended goodness. But in this fallen world, any such mirage shimmers and shakes as I approach it, only to dissipate if I do seem to grasp it in my hand. What is it, then, to be truly safe and sound? Is being *saved* synonymous, in this life singled out in Christ, with being *safe*? No, and yes.

Dostoevsky cites John 12:24 as the epigraph to his novel: "Verily, verily, I say unto you, Except a corn of wheat fall into the ground and die, it abideth alone: but if it die, it bringeth forth much fruit." An epigraph remains one of my favorite literary devices, perhaps because of how it so strategically yet subtly sets the context for the entire story. It plants a seed.

I placed Dostoevsky's book among my things in the suitcase and brought it back with me to England. It felt good to travel among such a brotherhood.

.ıllıllıı.

A few months later, after saying yes to God, I experienced what it meant to be "married" to Christ. I had come hesitantly to the altar when I came to think of having faith as a sort of "marriage." I had initially shuddered when I first heard of the church described as the "Bride of Christ." No matter how hard I tried, Gothic images of the "Bride of Frankenstein" instead flooded my brain: a woman with a tall black-and-gray-streaked beehive hairdo and skin as white as Saruman tottered toward me with zombie-like fixation. How to escape "the church"? I am sure many have thought the same from within the church and without. I am certainly not alone in the literalizing of metaphor. But when I pulled the cobwebs of "culturalese" aside and looked at the metaphor afresh, I saw instead how the "Bride of Christ" conveyed the relationship for each and every heart in love with Christ, and Christ's love for each and every heart, as a person, individually and as a people—*his* people. It didn't matter about the body, whether it had been used, abused, worn out, or looked through. It didn't matter if one was single or married, divorced or deserted. It didn't matter if one had been virgin or whore, celibate or sexually experienced, monogamous or polygamous. What mattered was the "upright heart and pure," as bound to God first and foremost, upon the recognition of sin and the asking of forgiveness, and then that becoming of a new creation and the living into that new and everlasting life.

Slowly, then, I began to see how there is no more precise metaphor for faith than marriage, the intimate binding of souls: the marriage of individuals, yes, but even more so, the marriage of one's own heart to Christ's. I began to see just why it was such a predominant metaphor in the Bible, representing the relationship between the Lord and his people. I grew to appreciate the intimacy of the God that knew my thoughts when no one else did—which, by the way, seemed a courteous privacy proof alone of grace. The Song of Songs sings out to each of us romantically and spiritually:

My beloved spoke and said to me,
"Arise, my darling,
    my beautiful one, come with me.
See! The winter is past;
    the rains are over and gone.
Flowers appear on the earth;
    the season of singing has come,
the cooing of doves
    is heard in our land."

As a newly single believer finding myself singular in Christ, I experienced a rich time when I was able to grow in God in a focused way and trust in his promises for me and me alone. I got to know many Christians who were single or married, who were widowed or divorced, all with different stories within his story but all, through their covenant with Christ, "married" to their Beloved, a love we all shared in communion and yet was intimately private for each believer. Singleness was not a default. Without God, we are isolated, no matter our status. In Emmanuel, however, none of us is alone.

I began to see, then, that the Christian, once a Christian, was already "married": that is, all decisions and actions were made in consideration of and deference to God, and that there was no one more just, merciful, or good. God was the partner I would now check in with first and foremost: the partner who loved me unconditionally regardless of my other worldly statuses, or lack thereof. This partner was by far my superior and yet fully entered my limitations, a friend closer than a brother, closer than a lover, who lived and died and lives still for me. The partner who assures me that regardless of circumstance, sin, and even doubt, he is with me always. In acknowledging myself as Christ's beloved and as part of his church, a single one of his people, a singular person made in his image, I had, well, married *way* up.

We speak of the single life, but rarely of the *singular*. In being already married as lovers of Christ who form his church, we are singularly sanctified. We are daringly safe. Being married to our Savior forms the foundational relationship of the life of the believer called to follow Christ. A marriage between believers offers the opportunity to extend this metaphor further—the central-most metaphor of the Bible—and so to provide another layer of its representation to a world much in need of such light. But for those of us for whom the greatest majority seem to be broken marriages not built on Christ, it is hard to see how even one's soul could be in intimate relationship with Another other than self, or how intimate relationship with Another could bring even more intimate understanding of self.

In her speech at the National Prayer Breakfast in 1994, the year that I left Canada for the United Kingdom, Mother Teresa told the memorable story of a poor Hindu family who shared their rice with an equally starving neighboring Muslim family. She explained how the Hindu children radiated the joy and peace shared with their mother because "she had the love to give until it hurts." Love begins, as Mother Teresa illustrates, in the family, and for those who profess to be followers of Christ, the family pertains to our conscientious legacy of loving as children of God. Of her love and lover, Mother Teresa concluded:

> Because I talk so much of giving with a smile, once a professor from the United States asked me: "Are you married?" And I said: "Yes, and I find it sometimes very difficult to smile at my spouse, Jesus, because He can be very demanding—sometimes." This is really something true. And this is where love comes in— when it is demanding, and yet we can give it with joy.

In this life singular, bound freely and forever to my Love, I am closest to my soundest when I ask to be disturbed.

Chapter Three

IT'S ALL RELATIVE

For we all were in that one man, since we all
were that one man, who fell into sin.

St. Augustine

I returned to Oxford University to start my second Michaelmas, or fall term, as a relatively new Christian in the fall of 1995. Over the summer, I had changed from Oriel College to St. Peter's College in order to begin a "student welfare" position. Jetlagged and in desperate need of good, strong, North American coffee for that morning of new beginnings, I stumbled into the front quad of St. Peter's, blinking my way to the porter's lodge. I struggled to bring my vision into focus; everything seemed wrapped in a fog. As I slowly grew more awake, braced by the chilly autumn morning air, I realized everything really *was* in a fog. The famed English mist clung everywhere, softening the lines of reality and giving me the impression of being newly wakened, still moving among dreams. I lamented not donning a scarf or gloves. The hazy promise of a sun beyond my dormer window had tricked me into thinking it would be warmer than it was. Returning to England from Canada took all sorts of adjustments, including seasonal. I came from a climate decisive in its changing seasons, but here, the fog undercut assumptions and blurred demarcations. In the short time it took me to reach the porter's lodge, my hair fell limp from the damp. *So much for trying to style it before heading out,* I thought to myself as I reached in my bag for a hair clip—the staple of any girl who often bends her head to read in the land of the fine-hair-challenging damp.

Entering the lively rush of the college porter's lodge always woke me up. A porter's lodge acts as a sort of antechamber to every Oxford college. While some are more cramped than others, they all offer a common place of communication with the sharing of news and distribution of gossip. They are lined with "pigeon holes," or small shelves or slots, one for each person associated with the college, where mail can be delivered or notes and small items left for pick up. There is also a desk or counter (usually behind a sliding glass window) where the porter—a sort of doorman who is also a jack-of-all-trades—keeps vigil and screens the constant onslaught of visitors flowing into the college while also addressing the various needs of those who belong to the college. A porter skillfully wears many hats: greeter, intimidator, administrator, postman, customs officer, security guard, bouncer, Sybil.

Since the only public entrance to any given college is through the porter's lodge, it is virtually impossible to sidestep a porter's scrutiny. Some larger or wealthier colleges may have a team of porters on at once, though usually there is a head day porter and a head night one. Regardless, as a member of a college, you get to know your porters very well, not only because you see them regularly but also because they make it their business to know your business. I could see how this may seem intrusive at first to the typical North American student who prefers—and indeed has been trained by our public school systems—to expect permissive anonymity rather than personal responsibility. But once I got over the initial shock of having my comings and goings so closely monitored, I began to own an increasing admiration for the porter's ability to know everyone's name, immediately recognize who should and shouldn't be there, and their very British bulldog protectiveness of the college and its grounds. I felt safer knowing that someone who truly loved the college and its members sat at its portals literally day and night. I also looked forward to the news updates from my porters and enjoyed their witty banter. Long after leaving Oxford, the interaction with a delightful porter remains one of the foremost things I miss. I still feel a sort of absence whenever I pass through the doorway of some grand academic building and fail to hear a cheerful greeting to my face or a warm benediction at my back.

Porter's lodges are a hive of activity, and it was no exception that morning. Having transferred to St. Peter's College for a student advisor and teaching position, I was entering my final year of the master of philosophy degree in Romantic literature. This would be an intense year, full of "A papers" (a set of concentrated essays on my subject matter) as well as final written exams, a full thesis, and a live verbal defense. I had my work cut out for me, and then some.

As one of the "younger" colleges, St. Peter's has a reputation for good sportsmanship, both in athleticism and demeanor. Its founding chapel dated to 1874, and the college that grew up around it was thereby referred to as New Inn Hall. It is a warm and friendly college marked by an unpretentiousness that comes with its higher percentage of scholarship students like me. I stopped at the lodge and checked my mail. I pulled out a wad of papers that had built up over the summer, mainly announcements of different events going on throughout the city. Luckily at the time, porters kept a keen eye on what was distributed and fliers were usually reserved to places where they could be posted, so there was very little junk mail. Still, there was usually correspondence from my scholarship providers and invitations to a gala, fundraiser, or friend's art show, music concert, or some other fete. Oxford's social schedule, especially during term, ran at an astounding pace.

Standing in the porter's lodge sifting through my backlog of mail, I spotted a note from Rachel, a friend of mine from my church in Oxford. She was inviting me to a "back to term" Bible study brunch at her course supervisor's home. I noted with dismay, however, that the date was *today*—the gathering would take place in about an hour, in fact. I had to admit, I didn't have anything on my agenda today. I had mentally penciled it in as an "adjustment day": a quiet day to take it easy and acclimate to the time change, to get ready for term and settled in a bit. I had planned a little reading, some errand running, and stockpiling of the usual student groceries such as ramen noodles and the very North American staple of peanut butter, jam, and bread. I looked over at our porter caught between a belligerent tourist insisting on his right to wander through and take photographs of the private residences, and someone who had parked his bicycle smack in the middle of the narrow doorway. I hadn't planned on Bible study—I wasn't really sure if I was the Bible Study Type. I found myself oddly inconvenienced that I still had time to make the meeting. I started to crumple up Rachel's note in my fist, preparing to practice my aim and hit my mark in the trash bin at the other side of the lodge.

"So luv, where are you off to this fine morning?" the porter, having returned to his desk, chirped at me through the glass window. Only a Brit would call such a foggy morning "fine."

"To find a good cup of coffee," I answered him.

"Tea won't do?" he teased. "Coffee will still be on in the hall, too, you know." He nodded toward the college dining room.

"I said a *good* cup, Paul," I replied, smiling.

He chose to ignore my slight of a domestic "cuppa," as the Brits called it, instead replying while he continued to sort mail at his desk, "And *then* where are you headed?"

"Oh, perhaps for some reading at the Bodley; I need to get ready for term . . ." I got ready to raise my arm with my crumpled fastball.

Paul lifted his spectacles and looked down his nose at me. "If you walk lively, luv, you could still make your friend's invite."

I checked my arm in shock at his knowledge of my invitation, but then I lowered it knowingly. Having become more accustomed to Oxford student life by now, I knew any mock protest at my college porter's knowledge of my private life, including correspondence (that I had to admit was on a postcard, a common form of communication among students and faculty), would be useless. *Porters know everything.* It's really just a matter of whether they choose to let on that they know everything or not.

"Well?" he prompted.

"Oh, I'm not sure I'm up for it," I hedged, fiddling with my paper ball.

"Why not?" Porters can be ruthlessly nosy—especially Paul.

"Well, I'm tired, you know, Paul, after all I just got back in late yesterday, and then, well . . ." I tried moving closer to the door.

"Did you read the PS?" Paul's tone wouldn't let me go.

"The what?"

"The postscript, luv. What didya think?"

"Wait," I began. "You read my postscript?"

"No, hers."

It's useless to argue with a porter over information. Or over anything, for that matter. They hold the keys, literally, to everything. Not a small irony, either, to be lost on one when it came to the porter of St. Peter's College. The college shield itself bears the keys of St. Peter's. In this case, there was literally no use in robbing Peter to pay Paul. Paul already had the keys to it all.

"Well, go on, take a look, luv." Paul nodded then went back to his sorting. It *is* hard to be upset at someone who calls you "luv." I sighed and uncrumpled my postcard, smoothing it out so I could look down again at Rachel's gently looped handwriting, easy to read even without spectacles. *P.S. If nothing else, come for the coffee, Caro. I promise it will be good!*

"Very funny, Paul," I said as I turned to go.

"Cheers, luv." He smiled and waved as I slipped the note into my back pocket and stepped out of the porter's lodge into the midmorning hustle and bustle of the city center just outside St. Peter's gates. Out of habit now, I lifted my foot high over the doorway step, taking care not to stumble on the raised platform on my way into the street.

Oh, but it was good to be back in Oxford, England, in that incomparable city of dreaming spires! Although my homesickness for Canada still pierced my heart, especially at the parting from loved ones, the vibrant community I had come to grow and love at Oxford served as a balm. And there still remained nothing like reading works by the greatest minds in the human tradition amid glorious architecture often as old, if not older, than the classic works themselves. Just sitting in the Bodleian Library made one feel smart. With over eleven million items, it serves as the main research library of Oxford University and one of the oldest libraries in Europe, second only in size to the British Library. Everywhere in Oxford, the old stonewalls felt steeped with souls, the walkways seemed to wind through wisdom. What a glorious place to study, or as the Brits say, "read" a subject. And then to "read" literature, of all things—and then to have found faith, with a hope and a peace that are practical and very relevant, and yet which defy complete rational deduction or understanding. Almost a year ago, I had struggled against God among these hallowed halls, within these immaculate quads and walled gardens, and eventually became a Christian—not quite kicking and screaming, like how C. S. Lewis described his conversion as "the most reluctant convert in England"—but fairly close. It had been a good row: one that I had to admit, deep down, I hadn't wanted to win.

I strolled down High Street, the main road through Oxford, fondly referred to as "the High," enjoying the rush of busy lives around me, set to the backdrop of some of the most glorious architecture in the world. How oblivious familiarity makes us to that which, once removed, we would ache to have in our grasp! Students intent on making it to their tutorials on time whizzed past me on bicycles; dons preoccupied with working out an algorithm or giving a lecture walked briskly to their next appointment, some muttering to themselves with faces raised to the sky, others stooped over with heads bowed to the pavement. Rivulets of tourists trickled through the crowd of regulars, clicking cameras and stopping to browse postcard kiosks parked outside the various gift shops along the way. It can be like swimming upstream against salmon, traveling up the High. I finally arrived at the little greasy breakfast cafe in front of St. Edmund Hall, where I dashed in and asked for a coffee to go. I thought it best to be sure I got my java fix; I couldn't risk showing up to what might prove a friend's empty promise when it came to such an important addiction.

The server's surprise met with my own. He was completely aghast that I would want to drink hot coffee as I moved, let alone *out on the street.* This would be one of many culture shocks I would experience. This run-in reminded me of a conversation I had with Maria, an

Italian graduate student who had shared her befuddlement with me about getting coffee-to-go: "Why would you ever want to do that?" she said with some alarm. "Isn't coffee made better by conversation? Shouldn't you sit and savor it? Don't you want to watch people walk by? Is it not like wine, and made to sip slowly for a reason?"

I felt all the harried shame of my white-rabbit culture when I thought of Maria, dark-haired and even darker-eyed, full of stereotypical Italian passion—which is stereotypical with good reason—as I swallowed back the envy I had, as shared by the rest of the non-Italian human race, for all she embodied. Even if she did condescend to take a travel cup in her hand, it would slosh all over, given her gesticulating. No wonder drinking coffee involves setting down your cup in Italy—and settling yourself into the glorious reveling in resting, talking, and *enjoying* all of what such a seemingly simple act entails.

So, needless to say (and my, how this will date me further), I could not get a coffee-to-go back then at Oxford: this was pre-Starbucks era, in a galaxy far, far away . . . and perhaps it was an omen, I told myself grouchily that foggy morning. Maybe Bible study was for the birds.

Finding it hard to step lively through the heavy traffic without my caffeine fix, I did manage to cross the street for the pleasant walk along Magdalen Bridge to Headington, the suburb just up the hill from the city. After a long pilgrimage, I finally arrived at the address that Rachel gave in her note. I gave a timid knock on the door. No one answered. Engulfed in a sudden shyness that only heightened my trepidation, I waited the obligatory few moments, then began to back down the porch steps with, I had to admit, some relief. Just as I turned my back to commit foot to the sidewalk again, however, a friendly voice called out:

"Hey there! Sorry we didn't hear the door, lass. With everyone reuniting after summer vac, it's a bit chatty inside!"

I stopped in my tracks on the bottom step. He had me at "lass." Yeah, I am a sucker for brogues. I didn't say anything, however, and just stood there, looking up at the welcoming face of a tall, thin older man in the doorway. This must be Rachel's supervisor, I realized. Another one of those sly Christians . . . they are *everywhere*! They're like ninja darts of salt and light about to deploy upon my default of tasteless and darkling cynicism. Excuses as to why I couldn't stay began running through my head, but I stood paralyzed. I found it hard to think about lying and walking at the same time.

"You're Rachel's friend, aren't you?" he said, his dancing eyes studying me closely.

I nodded. The highlander extended his hand as he straddled down the steps toward me.

"Alastair. Lovely to meet you." His hand gripped mine with a firm kindness.

"Carolyn," I said as I shook his hand in return.

"I know. I've heard so many wonderful things about you! Welcome! We were hoping you'd make it," he said warmly.

I felt taken aback at having felt so taken aback. "I'm . . . uh . . . I don't think I can stay long," I stammered. Keeping my hand in his, he pulled me ever so subtly up a step.

"Stay as short or as long as you like," he replied. "But you must have a cup of our fantastic coffee. Especially on a morning like this, where you can barely see your hand in front of your face! We're not serving that instant stuff. One of our friends here brought coffee from her work in starting up fair trade in Guatemala. Ground fresh just now. A real treat! The aroma fills the house. Here, come closer, can you smell it?"

I stood in the doorway now, and yes, I could smell it. For a jet-lagged, fog-drenched, caffeine-craving North American early in the morning, he had me hooked. Further.

"We have fresh scones, too, and jam." He winked.

Fisher of (wo)men, indeed. *Man, those Christians are sneaky,* I found myself thinking as I climbed the last step, hungry and thirsty, I had to admit, for so much more than scones and coffee.

Wait. I stopped in the doorway. *Those Christians*—I now realized that included me.

"*We* have . . ."

We? The French pun on *yes* was not lost on a bilingual Canadian girl like me.

"Come, warm yourself. We are gathered in the kitchen by the wood stove." Alastair held the door open wide for me. "Rachel will be delighted you made it. She was hoping you'd received her note in time."

As I passed through the doorway to the St. Ebbe's Bible Study, people came up to greet me, took my jacket, relieved me of my always-heavy book bag, and directed me to the warm circle of laughter around a table laden with baked goods fresh from the oven. Someone handed me a steaming cup of delicious-smelling coffee, someone else a still-warm scone with jam on a very old chipped china plate—more beautiful for the chip, and the age. A seat was pulled back for me, a space made, expectant, waiting to be filled, fulfilling. My cup overflows among such kin at the table of, in the presence of, our Father.

"Faithless is he that says farewell when the road darkens," wrote J. R. R. Tolkien in his legendary literary work *The Fellowship of the Ring*. For those of us who know what it is like to travel through life without fellowship, the lonely road is dark indeed. Like many in North America, I grew up in a loosely "Christian" home, with some of the boundaries of an orthodox tradition but none of the explanations. When my grandparents were alive, we attended church for special occasions such as Christmas and Easter, but as the older generation passed on and my mother struggled to raise us as a single parent, any churchgoing fell away. I simply didn't know how to *be* in a room full of Christians.

Turns out, at that first Bible study gathering, I was the last one to leave. Having enjoyed myself completely, I lingered to talk with the assistant pastor of St. Ebbe's, a thoughtful and engaging man. Throughout the entire study, as a group gathered in God's name, no topic was off limits, no problem too big to ask for support, no prayer request too small to lift up. The conversation kited high and low through laughter and tears, jokes and concerns. We read and discussed Scripture, and we read and discussed ourselves. I realized right then and there that people hesitate about religion because they think it is not relevant to their own lives. Cultivating and experiencing fellowship bears testimony to the relevance of reverence.

In *The City of God,* St. Augustine considers the propagation of both families in terms of the spiritual and the earthly cities. The spiritual city consists of those who live by faith, who seek righteousness as a means of serving God because they genuinely love him and rest in his love for them. The earthly city, in contrast, comprises those who live according to themselves: those driven solely by their own needs, wants, lusts, and interests without the perspective, courage, and wisdom afforded by faith—hope in things unseen. As early as Genesis, Augustine illustrated, we see the origination of these two different ways of being: "Of these two first parents of the human race, then, Cain was the firstborn, and he belonged to the city of men; after him was born Abel, who belonged to the city of God." Cain slays Abel, and the story, Augustine went on to explain, shows us how each man, "being derived from condemned stock, is first of all born of Adam evil and carnal, and becomes good and spiritual only afterward, when he is grafted into Christ by regeneration: so was it in the human race as a whole." We are related in sin, and we are related in re-demption. Life along this spectrum, indeed, is relative to what, and Whom, we believe.

"The first founder of the earthly city, then, was a fratricide," Augustine said of Cain. This statement stopped me in my tracks. As did Augustine's analysis of how this archetype of crime sits at the foundation of life and the system of lives lived without God. Instantly, the fallen world around me, in all of its senseless violence, illness, and betrayals, made sense—or, rather, as much sense as was possible on this side of looking into a glass darkly. We are not our brother's keeper because we are not a keeper of our promises. But we are our brother's keeper as reflections of our common maker. We see this same witness in our being made in the image of God, and how this testimony carries, quite literally, in our successive reflections of our ancestors. DNA twines our being made in the image of God, and this image is passed down through the generations. We bear witness all the way back to our beginnings. Our individual genes speak of our common Genesis.

In Acts, we have a double testimony: Saul, before he is Paul, witnesses the testimony of Stephen to Christ. Paul would have heard Stephen skillfully lead his listeners through Jewish history. Stephen tells how Abraham fathered Isaac, and Isaac fathered Jacob, and Jacob became the father of the twelve patriarchs. Stephen tells a story from the past, but also gives a template for the present and the future too. Stephen's tracing of Jesus' lineage in Saul's presence essentially amounts to a history of sex. Sons are named and fathers are identified; daughters, too, even in a patriarchal society, have significant roles to play. And in God's economy, arguably the most important roles are played by women. Families are mapped out from the beginning of time. Our collective family tree as a human race takes on shape and meaning, especially as we begin to see how some branches come forth by birth and others grafted in by adoption, but all by rebirth into God's family: "for we are members of [Christ's] body." The family tree has its roots, literally, in the tree of the knowledge of good and evil in Eden, vining throughout the ages and embodying all prophesy into the cross, or tree, on which Jesus hung, pointing to the tree of life in the final book of Revelation: "On each side of the river stood the tree of life, bearing twelve crops of fruit, yielding its fruit every month. And the leaves of the tree are for the healing of the nations." The entire family will be gathered and the whole world shall be healed.

Comparing just the books of Genesis and Acts shows how inter-related genealogy is with spirituality; the blood of Christ runs in the veins of redeemed creation. Genealogy is such an important detail in Scripture because it displays the intricacy of fulfilled prophecy. It emphasizes family and shows God at work right down to the very details of our DNA. But blood is not all. Faith runs deeper than bi-ology. We are children of God twice over, by creation and by adoption: by having been made in his image, and having come to know how we are reborn in his grace. The Bible takes our under-standing of family to show us what real family is. We are set within specific relationships, spaces, places, and times, and yet we are eternal, limitless, and loved beyond comprehension.

Sex as the template for genealogy is important because sexuality is a reflection of God's relationship with us. Our relationship to sex speaks of our relationship to God. And because our relationship with God must precede our relationship with everything else, including our own selves, working from this first relationship changes every-thing. As a result, more often than not in a culture that neglects our dignity as spiritual beings, pursuing this foundational relationship can feel countercultural, though it is God's norm, for in becoming children of God we become who he intended us to be.

We are in relationship to everything, with far-reaching effects from the personal to the global, as J. Richard Middleton reminds us: "I am *in relationship* not just to other persons, but also to social and political institutions, to traditions, to the environment"—essentially, to everything. I had never really considered the significance of "relations" before becoming a person of faith, let alone asked such questions of my responsibility within and to such relationships. Fellowship reminds us of our inextricability from relationship. As a commandment to love one another, it runs deeper and higher and harder and purer. Fellowship stems from being family in God. Fellowship is patient and constant and committed. Fellowship says you must love me, even when you are not in the mood. Fellowship replies that I must love you, even when I'm not in the mood. Fellowship is inconvenient, accountable, comfortably and uncomfortably kind. Fellowship offers a safe place to land. You can be friends since birth with someone and have years of history together, but if one knows Christ and the other doesn't, there exists a "shining barrier" through which there can never quite be a full connection because one lives by the promise, knows of the hope, and trusts in the giver in a way that the other cannot perceive, live by, or understand.

The difference between "conversion" and "conversation" really does involve where a soul is "at." One has an eternal point of view; the other, simply, does not. One owns a hope that runs deeper than feeling or character; the other does not. But two strangers who know and love Christ from opposite ends of the earth (or Middle-Earth!) can meet and have instantaneous fellowship. They share the same frame of reference, the same heart language (even if their mother tongues differ). They have been grafted to the same tree, watered by the same spring, sustained by the same roots, and branch toward the same heaven. They know of whence the other speaks and journey toward the same home together. Through the suffering shared or the pain understood runs a golden thread binding them in the promise that nothing, not a thing, lies outside of the redemptive power of God. And that all, indeed, will be well.

Friends in fellowship, family in faith, must be the greatest blessing on this side of heaven, the greatest foretaste of the ultimate gathering. Begotten by the loving and perfect will of God, and being among those who share this birthright and remind me of my own, has a way of changing the undercurrent of a conversation. It also creates such good fire-filled company as to keep the road ahead well lit.

Chapter Four

PREMARITAL SECTS

*Indeed, this is already sin, to desire those things which the
law of God forbids, and to abstain from them through
fear of punishment, not through love of righteousness.*

St. Augustine

The snow surprised us. As did,
later, the stars, which showed up
once the curtain of snow pulled back, in time to sing for their supper.

What I didn't realize at the time was that the snow and the stars
and the surprise were always there and intermingled. And that obedience is preferred to sacrifice, and yet often they are one and the
same: these two, these too, intermingled.

During my studies abroad, I always came home for the holidays,
but this year I had stayed in England longer than planned. After becoming a Christian, breaking up with my fiancé, and finishing my
master's degree, I applied to do my doctorate whilst starting a
teaching career in the United Kingdom. It looked more and more like
England would be my permanent residence, at least for the fore-
seeable future, but Canada would always feel like home and so I

returned there once again. The TV weatherman, with all the cunning confidence of an itinerant selling tonic, had proclaimed an absolutely snowless week ahead. The forecast called for cold—just cold—and it was the sheer and pure kind of cold, so perfect as to almost seem manufactured, like the inside of a hockey arena, where it hurts to breathe deeply unless you are sweating with exertion: nostril-sticking, lung burning, ear-biting cold. After years of living in England, I had almost forgotten how determined Canadian seasons could be in their distinction from each other.

In England, seasons had blurred one into the other with a genteel smoothing over of rain. Paisley frost covered the college window-panes with a wild politeness, like the morning fruition of a nocturnal Coleridge poem. Winter cold settled in as a constant chill, both inside and outside of the building, where often the only circle of grace was immediately in front of the fire (since almost every room there still had a fireplace, or if you were in a more "modern" abode— *modern* being a relative term in England—you were warmed by a hissing radiator). Folks there referred to *damp* not as a condition or adjective, but more like a noun, personified, deserving of its own respect and tolerances—like a nodding deference to one's sweet but addled old aunt who lived with the family for as long as anyone could remember but who wasn't really any bother unless she wandered around at inopportune times. "Mind the damp," my friend who lived in the Cotswolds would say to me with a certain apologetic fondness whenever I stayed in her little guest room on the other end of house far from the wood stove on which she dried her laundry, as if I had to sidestep some genteel inconvenience or tolerate some pesky ghost.

In Canada, however, the frost knows no such demure constraints; it does not inhabit as a being bent over a cane muddling somewhere between dank warmth and fusty chill. In my hometown of London,

Ontario, this winter "damp" was no dame. Rather, the cold slices through you like the edge of a blade; snow swirls with the ferocity of a bull enraged by a matador whipping a white cape. For white everything is, becomes, and stays, until it dirties into gray before "the brown brink eastward, springs" at the dawn of summer solstice. In the land of my birth, one could fall asleep to a lone snowflake or two drifting outside the window and open your eyes in the morning to a world washed in white and so still as to shatter your assumption that you awoke alive.

Around midnight, as I sat reading Lord Byron for my thesis, our furnace groaned and then gasped its last. A few hours later, I woke to frost on the inside of my window. With our budget tight, we had to sit tight, too, until an affordable repairman could be found, never a small feat. Meanwhile mom left early for work and once my sister realized the pilot also affected our hot water, she immediately abandoned me for her boyfriend's warmer home claiming she had to wash her hair or she'd *die*. I would not be flying back to England for a few weeks yet, being on the longer "vac" from Oxford, so I offered to stay put, research repairmen, and then wait for the service call.

The house was growing colder by the minute, so I put on another layer of clothes along with the kettle. Living in England prepared one for all sorts of life situations, I had found. A cuppa solved just about anything, according to the Brits.

By mid-morning, I had finally located a repairman within our budget. This came with one small glitch, however. He wouldn't be able to show up for an estimate until the evening after tomorrow. There was a *small chance,* however, the secretary on the other end of the phone emphasized, that someone may be able to come by before then, but it would be a last-minute appointment. If no one answered the door when he knocked, they would cancel and we'd have to rebook.

"So essentially I have to wait here for two days in a freezing house on the off chance that someone from your company can come by?" I clarified over the phone, my voice tight with restrained irritation. "But—and let me get this straight—the earliest they can come is by tomorrow evening. But if they do come any earlier, and I happen to miss the doorbell, they won't come back at all?"

"That's correct," she replied even more coolly than my house was becoming. "We need to confirm the call."

"I am confirming the call," I told her. "Right now, talking with you."

"No, not this call on the phone," she replied. "The call to the house."

"I see. Could you give me a window? I mean, something a bit more specific than, say, a forty-eight-hour span?"

"No, this is the best we can do," she replied matter-of-factly. I imagined her in a sleeveless blouse, taking calls from some remote tropical location.

I glanced at their slogan on the phonebook page on the counter in front of me: *Don't be left in the cold! We are here to meet any budget!*

Some budgets are met later than others, I saw clearly now. But I refrained from saying so and instead managed a tight "thank you." Repair companies hold such unfair sway. How assertive can one risk being when faced with a cold shower in frigid air?

.ılıllıı.

I had just celebrated my second Christmas as a Christian. An "un-yoked" Christian, that is . . . married to Christ, true, but not dating or involved or committed to any son of Adam. I had taken a long, deliberate break from men. Sure, I had dated a few times since my breakup with my college sweetheart, but nothing serious. I realized that good men, let alone good Christian men, were indeed hard to find, especially in academia. The pickings seemed slim from the Tree of Life.

As a result, I had been drawn to men with "spiritual bents" at least. I reasoned to myself that there might be wiggle room to grow together, though wiggle into which room, who knew. Atheists were off the table: too certain about being certain, and no starting reference point, I found. I listened and listened all evening to one self-professed atheist I ended up going out with in a moment of weakness (it didn't help that he was easy on the eyes).

"The resurrection—what a crock of . . ." he declared over drinks.

"How do you know?" I replied.

"No one saw it," he said simply.

"Saw what?"

"You know, *it.*"

"The missing body?" I asked, trying to wade through the wide, sweeping dismissal.

"Yeah, that's it."

"Isn't 'it' missing the point?" I asked.

"It's about things you can see, my dear." He ordered me another glass of wine. I looked out the pub window at his Aston Martin parked outside—not the red one, as he had decided to take the black. *Seeing is believing, indeed,* I had to admit.

"Christianity is such a conspiracy," he said. "Now take dinosaurs. They clearly existed."

"No one has seen a dinosaur either," I replied.

"They are reconstructed," he stated.

"From what, really?" I couldn't help myself.

"Fossils. Bones. Archeological materials. Where have you been?" He peered at me through his beer goggles. With a sigh, I knew he wouldn't be driving me back to the college.

"If we are talking about conspiracies, the idea of them sure sells a lot of children's products." I settled back in my pub bench.

"So, what are you saying?" He looked at me as steadily as he could.

"Well," I shrugged, "let's just say I find the existence of an ark that is minutely described in detail in a historical text to be far more compelling than a huge lizard projected through a great big cash-hungry game of connect the dots."

He looked at me, aghast. Clearly, he had been an ardent lover of dinosaurs as a kid. I knew I was exaggerating a little, but still, I felt like archeology or science or medicine are always fodder for atheists' arguments until you try applying them to biblical considerations. Increasingly, I found the modern discoveries and the Bible not to be at odds—in fact, quite the opposite.

"There is no such thing as the unseen," he declared as he pulled himself up straight. "Everything can be explained, by any of us, with enough research and persistence."

I seriously weighed living compatibly with this attitude. It would come with living with not one, but *two* Aston Martins, after all. But I still found myself mumbling Shakespeare under my breath, "There are more things in heaven and earth, Horatio, than are dreamt of in your philosophy."

Next, I dated a Mormon. He was a lovely guy; earnest and upright. We drank water at dinner. No alcohol. Not even caffeine. Despite the summer heat, he wore scratchy long underwear to remind him of his penitence. I found myself wondering, *had Jesus not died on the cross for irritation too?*

A Buddhist took me for a beautiful outing on the river. We enjoyed a walk together along the bank. He was lovely and accepting; at peace with himself and at peace with me and with all about him. He trusted in karma, he told me, the law that every cause has an effect. This simple law, he explained, dictates why inequality exists; people bring on themselves their own shortcomings and struggles, their own successes and wealth. Karma underlines the importance of all individuals being responsible for their past and present actions. While I was drawn to the acceptance of others and the search for wisdom, I just couldn't reconcile myself to the notion of a cosmic boomerang ricocheting off multiple lives until we "got it right." Grace seemed to me to trump karma, and trusting my eternal life to this hunch, I politely declined another date. I figured such charity would simply come back to me if I were misled.

As an unbeliever first looking into the Christian faith, I used to be bothered by the apostle Paul's teaching, "Do not be yoked together with unbelievers. For what do righteousness and wickedness have in common? Or what fellowship can light have with darkness?" What right did this guy have to call people like me wicked or dark? How could it possibly be such a great iniquity to hang out with folks of all stripes? But as I grew to know Paul better—and through him, Jesus— I began to realize that they both hung out regularly with folks of all stripes. And as I grew in my faith, I realized, too, just what sinners we all are, and especially the darkness of my own heart. When it came to intermingling so that bodies and hearts and lives became one, wasn't it much better to at least start out on even spiritual footing, if you had the conscientious opportunity? Those who don't know any better simply don't know any better, and the Bible excuses them. But those who do, well, *do*. And the Bible holds them to a different accountability, and, if I am to be apologetically unapologetic, a higher bar.

"Unequally yoked" is another of the New Testament's agricultural metaphors that would have spoken to its audience at the time. A yoke joins two oxen to each other and to the burden they share. If equally yoked, the burden is distributed effectively and the oxen can get the work done, so to speak, or reach their destination and in particular, till their ground (incidentally, they work as a pair like Adam and Eve first did to work the ground for their survival in the fallen world). If unequally yoked, however—in the case where one ox is strong and the other is weaker—the weaker ox would walk more slowly than the stronger one, causing the load to go around in circles. They wouldn't get anywhere. And they would remain at odds with each other.

At some point in each date with a believer of another religious stripe, this metaphor, as off-putting as it may seem, did give me pause. The truth is not always comfortable. But it is a heck of a lot more comfortable than bearing an unequal yoke, and a lot less disorienting than going in circles. When we are yoked to Christ first, we gain our traction and purpose with peace (which is not the same as ease on this side of heaven, but it makes all the difference when you don't have it). Jesus says, "my yoke is easy and my burden light." But if I were honest, there was another niggling reason why these other men just didn't sit well in my yoke. It's because they didn't share their own yokes with Jesus, like I did. And for all the explaining, rationalizing, argumentation, and even well-intentioned kindness, they didn't live by the really real of Jesus. There existed, to use Sheldon Vanauken's illustration, a "shining barrier" between us—that line in the sand that Augustine identified as separating the two cities of all humankind. Without Spirit calling to Spirit, or deep to deep, between us, there would always be the lack of something between us. Believers and unbelievers are not necessarily at odds, as Augustine identified long ago: "The earthly city, which does not live by faith, seeks an earthly peace, and the end it proposes, in the well-ordered concord of civic obedience and rule, is the combination of men's wills to attain the things which are helpful to this life. The heavenly city, or rather the part of it which sojourns on earth and lives by faith, makes use of this peace only because it must, until this mortal condition which necessitates it shall pass away." We all use the same earthly means. What varies, however, is the heavenly end. Teleology makes all the difference. As a result, as J. Richard Middleton put it, "Ethics is lived eschatology."

I found myself thinking of the many long conversations about such faith-related topics back in my Oriel College dorm I had enjoyed with Theology Man, who my father had asked about, and who still, I had to admit, haunted my thoughts, though I was pretty sure I would never him see again. TDH (Tall, Dark, and Handsome) epitomized someone truly trying to follow Christ. He treated me, and women in general, with respect and dignity. Of course, he was far from perfect, but he spoke honestly with me about his struggles to remain committed to Christ first, especially in his sexual desires, and how he had to trust that God's design for sexual purity and for singleness or for marriage, if it should happen, had a very specific purpose. He was *different*—profoundly different—from any other man I had hitherto known. Along with other Christian friends I made, TDH and I discussed works such as C. S. Lewis's enduring *Mere Christianity* together. What was this "abundant life" I kept hearing about? The phrase rang of one of those empty Christianese clichéd terms, like "blessed assurance." *What on earth?* I used to wonder as an unbeliever. Sometimes life stinks, true, and anything by comparison would seem better. But sometimes life skips along pretty comfortably. Things are, well, good enough. And if, for instance, I have to admit there is something to this Christian life, but my significant other is not that interested, who cares? Live and let live. But what *is* living?

TDH used to say that the question mark sums up faith, since we are called to live in the mystery. Answers in and of themselves will never be enough. Proverbs 3:5-6 had been my Bible study group's chosen verse for the past academic year: "Trust in the Lord with all your heart and lean not on your own understanding; in all your ways submit to him, and he will make your paths straight." Faith and obedience. The two are often interchangeable forms of each other. We answer to God's faithfulness with our own, or at least our trying. But one day we will see God face-to-face, all will be put right, and every tear will be wiped away. The question mark will be replaced with the exclamation mark, and all will be glory! The reality, and beauty, and grace of the abundant life promised and modeled and offered through Christ hit me like a ton of butterflies, not bricks.

Speaking of butterflies, I found myself studying the card emblazoned with a monarch butterfly that I was using as a bookmark. I love butterflies, which the sender knew. Inside the card was a single question mark. Since TDH had left Oxford to pursue his career back in the United States, such beautiful cards had periodically found their way to me, always with the same message, a simple question mark:

?

I had just snipped off the tips of my gloves so I could turn the pages of my assigned reading when I heard the doorbell ring. It must be the repairman! I rejoiced at the thought of room temperature and bounded down the stairs to let him in.

.ılıllıı.

When I swung the door open into equally chilly air, a familiar face met me that appeared unfamiliar, however, in the fact of my doorframe. I stood speechless with surprise (no easy feat to achieve on me).

"Caro!" he called out, stepping forward to enclose me in a huge bear hug.

"Edward?" my surprised response came out muffled with my face pressed into his thick winter coat.

I stepped back and looked up at him. "What are you doing . . . *here*?!"

"I had your address from your Christmas card last year, and I thought I'd drop by."

"Drop by? From Oxford?" I still stood there in disbelief, forgetting to invite him in.

"No, silly. From Toronto. I was supposed to go see family in the States, remember?"

"Yes, okay, that's right . . ."

"My aunt and uncle, actually, but they had a big fight and well, they are separated, at least temporarily, but they put the house up for sale, and my uncle warned me it might have to be shown and I felt awkward about staying at my aunt's place because she is with her sister, who I met once at a party and well, it didn't really go well and I never called her back and—"

"Okay, Eddie, I get it. So why are you here?"

"Oh right. So I ended up in Toronto instead because I could change my flight from New York to there without charge, and my old roommate, Bernard, is working on Bloor Street now, he's a big shot, you know—"

"Right, right, and . . ." I gestured to "here," pointing at my front door with my finger.

"And so he had to come into London for a client and I bummed a ride with him, thinking I would pop around and see you. Bernie says it shouldn't snow, so he could drop me for a bit and then see his client and then drive back around to pick me up later, or both of us, if you want to go out on the town—"

"I smell snow," I cut him off.

"None's expected. Sky looks clear." Edward squinted up at the sky.

"What do you know about snow?" I teased him. "You're Australian."

He stepped inside, peeling off his jacket and passing it to me.

"Oh, wait," I said, passing it back. He looked hurt.

"Of course, you can stay!" I laughed at his Eeyore eyes. "But you might want to wear this." I rushed on to explain about our furnace's cardiac arrest. He grinned.

"I'm stuck here now until the repairman comes," I added glumly.

"I'll wait with you, then," Edward offered. He stepped closer. "So . . . it's just us?"

Suddenly, I wasn't so sure that was a good idea.

"I need to get through my reading list," I announced squarely.

"You still have some time," Edward moved closer still.

"It's been busy with Christmas, and, well, everything . . ." my frosty mist of breath mingled with his.

"I brought a book I need to get through in my backpack," Edward countered. "How about we read together on the couch? Just until the repairman arrives or your mom gets home? Or until Bernie circles back? It shouldn't take long until we get someone's car. Then we can go out if you want, grab a bite?"

"Sure," I smiled, inwardly scolding myself for being so presumptuous. It was Edward, for crying out loud. Eddie. We were friends. A few snowflakes slow-stepped in the transom above us.

"Coffee?" I asked.

"Cheers." He looked around. "I'll get some blankets for the couch. It feels like it's twenty below in here. How do you bloody Canadians do it?"

I went back into the kitchen.

"Oh I know," Edward called out after me, "Igloo lovin.'" He laughed at his own joke.

"Why does everyone else in the world believe that Canadians actually live in igloos?" I called back, irritated.

"Oh sorry, luv," Edward quickly answered, schmoozing. "We actually know that you only use them for special occasions. Besides, you have your faith to keep you all warm and fuzzy, right?"

I put on a strong pot of coffee. Through the kitchen window, I noticed that the previously blue sky had now colored into bone, and drifting tufts of snow replaced the flakes.

"It's starting to come down out there," I called out. I could hear Edward shuffling around upstairs for some blankets, then the creak on the stairs of his descent.

Edward finally answered from the living room, "Oh, it will pass. The guy on the radio in the car said no accumulation, if any at all."

Whatever, I thought. Who listens to a Canadian weather report anyway? We remained tied to our British roots on that front. By the time the coffee pot hissed its finish, the snow was coming down in torrents, erasing the roads in a matter of minutes. Edward and I continued to face each other whilst leaning on the counter, enjoying our witty banter. I surprised myself at just how attracted I felt to him. I mean it was goofball *Eddie*, after all, and an infamous ladies' man to boot. This will pass, I told myself. Like the snow coming down outside. Any brief longing is just from being too solitary. It's from studying too hard. It's from pent up sexual tension. It's from the caffeine and the cold.

There had always been some kind of spark between Edward and me, if I were honest, though until now I had chalked it up to the sort of charming and harmless flirting that often happened within the hallowed halls of Oxford between students who had enjoyed perhaps a little too much sherry at a college event. Besides, Edward was such a *player*—although I knew he owned a very sensitive and sincere side. He had lost his mother at a young age, and I also knew this loss had wounded him deeply. Oh, he was Rochester and Heathcliff and Byron all rolled up into one: mad, bad, and dangerous to know, with an Aussie accent and a flint-quick wit. And, oh my, he was a drop-dead gorgeous dresser: clothes do make the man. With all of the above, I had dared to open the door and invite him in! Anyone knows that the devil can only enter by invitation. Or was that the vampire? I argued it back and forth in my head as my thoughts slowly began to wonder what it would be like to have Edward kiss my neck . . .

The phone began ringing, one call after another, startling me back to reality. First, it was Edward's ride saying how the freeway was backed up and he wouldn't be back in town now for several hours. Then my mom called to say she would stay on at work until the snow-plows had made their rounds on the smaller campus roads she needed to navigate back to our place. My sister left her voicemail during my mom's call informing us she would stay through dinner at her boy-friend's; his dad would drive her home later in his much more winter-reliable car. After talking with my mom and then listening to my sister's message, I set down the receiver with unsteady hand. Edward, who overheard everything, gave me a look with an arched brow.

"What?" I shot at him. He shrugged and then started whistling "Let It Snow."

I reached for two mugs and poured coffee with a little milk into each. I decided to leave the milk on the counter, as there was no point in putting it back in the fridge. Edward stood across from me in the kitchen, leaning against the doorway with his cowboy-like composure. A reddish-blond Marlboro man, he appeared all confidence, the personification of Manifest Destiny. Or perhaps I should say, more akin to a meaty entrée at Outback Steakhouse, with a bloomin' onion side. I held out one mug to him.

Our fingertips touched and in spite of myself, I betrayed a swift intake of breath. Maybe it was that Commonwealth connection? He did have an accent to die for . . . the room suddenly seemed short on oxygen. I took a gulp of my coffee only to realize that I hadn't made it strong enough. We set down our cups in unison.

Edward looked at me strangely. I had never noticed before just what an unusual color of gray his eyes were: stormy, like him. His face crinkled with laugh lines. I recognized how the one corner of his mouth lifted when he was about to say something: a merry cynic, he.

My heart skipped a beat. I stood frozen to the spot—not just because of the broken furnace.

"So?" he finally said, more like an invitation than a pause.

"So," I echoed, leaning back against the counter. I was finding it hard to stand.

He stepped forward, closing the space between us. *Mind the gap!* I heard the English phrase reverberating somewhere in the back of my mind.

"I decided to leave the blankets on the bed," Edward whispered as he took my hand.

Oh the weather inside is frightful . . .

.ıllıllıı.

On that dark winter afternoon, in the sullied aftermath of Christmas when the tree sat forlorn in the corner and the gifts had been given and all that was left was to wait for the new year in anticipation or dread, I dragged the blankets off the bed upstairs and piled them on the living room couch instead. As I went to put more wood on the fire, Edward nestled himself into the couch and then poked his tousled head out of the covers. He gave me a playful grin.

"Come on in," he said as he lifted up the blanket and patted the space beside him. "The water's fine." He grinned like a Cheshire cat. Inside, under the blankets, sparks of static electricity glittered in the darkness every time we moved. Outside, the snow swirled, and my head with it. Inside, the two of us snuggled into our snow globe world, figurines in an ice castle shaken to blurry transparency. Outside,

Among twenty snowy mountains,
The only moving thing
Was the eye of the blackbird.

By the grace of God, the kind you only see in retrospect, we were wearing a lot of clothes, layers and layers in fact, because of the outside cold inside. But then it occurred to me that regardless of weather, people wore a lot of clothes in Shakespeare's time too, and that didn't seem to slow anyone down very much (hence the token bastard in almost every play). I pulled my turtleneck up around my ears. *How could I be in this position?* I inwardly chastised myself. I noticed our bodies indeed generated a lot of heat inside our couch cocoon. Other than the occasional trip to the hearth to put another log on the fire, we remained cozied together against the sting of the outer air.

We talked about all sorts of things: I chatted away about eccentric professors and the courses I was preparing to teach. Edward spoke about his plans to start a company in Australia after his graduation, and his struggle to quit smoking, and the tattoo he got as a Christmas gift to himself.

"Want to see it?" he innocently asked.

"Sure," I replied, intrigued . . . until I saw him begin to unzip his pants.

"Oh, that's okay, you can just describe it to me," I added quickly.

"Words could never do it justice, luv." He gave me a playful glance.

We talked about his childhood memories of his mom before she died, and of his decision to go to a grief support group. I found myself intensely enjoying his company again, as I had so many times before, and wondered to myself if I had in fact done the right thing in not dating him after all. But what did it matter now, I told myself, and surely there are more Christian men out there than TDH, and surely, they are not all eunuchs or awkward dancers? And yet the consideration of my faith between Eddie and me grew smaller and smaller until it seemed more like a pebble in my shoe: a small sore irritant at the base of my being whenever I tried to take a step forward with men.

"So, are you sure you're still a Christian then, Caro?" he said to me without warning and with a casually accusing tone, as though asking if I was over a bad cold before he sat too close to me.

"Yes, I am, Eddie." I replied, and meant it: an inconvenient truth. I was startled and a bit afraid, of what I wasn't quite sure. Rejection, perhaps? Mockery? That didn't make sense, as we had an electric friendship, though not a dating one. Yet his opinion mattered to me. Relief, however, also washed in, relief from the weight of small talk, of anything-but-God talk. The liberation of Truth-Talk.

"And you are sure this is what you want to be, how you want to live the rest of your life?" He studied me closely.

"Yes, this is how I want to live my life." The flames rolled closely around the log.

"Why?" he asked.

I sighed. "I've explained all this to you before, Edward."

"I know. I want to hear it again. I want to hear more of it."

Surprised, I tried making out his face, but the room was growing more shadowed in the shortened winter daylight. We sat together in the darkening quiet, with only the crackle of the fire between us.

"Tell me again." His voice seemed so plaintive and small that it startled me. I looked at his dear face and took a deep breath.

"Edward, I believe Jesus is who he said he was."

"But with so many rules and regulations, with such self-denial?" Edward insisted.

"Well, I suspect you are kicking against organized religion, just like I did, and still do at times, Eddie. Or that you are caught up about what people and institutions spin about Jesus. I struggle with that too. So many judgments and so little grace! But if you knew Jesus himself, what he actually said and taught and did, and who he was, you may see it differently."

"Do you have anything to drink?" he asked, suddenly changing the topic. "Not coffee. Something stronger."

I wavered. A few bottles of leftover Christmas cheer remained in the living room cupboard, almost within reach but just out of view. I felt a lot of things at once, and I guessed that adding spirits to the Holy Spirit might be a dangerous combination. I needed a clear head. But what about a clear heart? That seemed impossible with all these emotions . . . all this longing, and need, and lust, and curiosity, and compassion, and frustration, and . . .

Eddie rubbed his hands in anticipation as I continued to hesitate. Maybe the head and the heart don't have to be so separated after all? Maybe bringing them together is what faith allows us to do, and what prayer encourages, and what wisdom entails? Eddie and I had shared many drinks in the past. Perhaps it was time, however, to revisit such a conversation *ex vino veritas* instead. Just as C. S. Lewis reminded us, "the ancient Persians debated everything twice: once when they were drunk and once when they were sober."

"No," I finally replied.

Edward remained silent.

"Obedience is a way of showing one's love for God," I replied to his silence. "Because God desires our obedience since he's set out the ways for us to better know and experience his love."

"In a sense, then, the rules are freeing . . ." Edward pondered out loud.

"Yes, I would agree. I see them more as reminders about what is best for me, and for others, in spite of me."

"But how can you be sure about what you believe?" Edward asked.

Being the obnoxious zealot I must have appeared to be, I quoted Hebrews 11:1 to him, "Now faith is confidence in what we hope for and assurance in what we do not see." I meant it sincerely, but Edward threw me a confused look.

I caught myself. "I'm sorry. I know. I just love that verse, though I'm beginning to sound like one of those wackos who answers every question with a quote from the Bible."

"There's a lot your faith doesn't let you see," he said with a wry smile.

"Touché," I conceded. "I guess your tattoo will have to wait until revelation."

"On the other side of heaven, baby," Edward touched my cheek.

He looked relieved. Maybe he, too, was tired of the small talk, or at least, smaller talk? Maybe we all are. Maybe one of the blessings of Scripture, actually, is that it's anything but small. It's just our clichéd talk of it that makes it seem so. Fear is a petty master. It has a way of making great things appear insignificant, and often the opposite as well.

"Now faith is confidence in what we hope for and assurance in what we do not see," Edward repeated slowly.

"Eddie, in all seriousness, I'm really getting those kind of quotations—I mean, I understand them, or at least have a sense of the bigger thing they point to. They get tossed around in our culture, sure, but they really do say something. They say it better than I ever could. I think they've hung around for a reason."

"True," Edward conceded. "It's just a shame that they get tossed as barbs or judgments."

"Yes," I agreed. "But other times people have no idea they are even quoting Scripture. It just seems that the power of it goes unrecognized, even exploited, if there isn't some personal connection through faith."

"Fair point," Edward replied. "But what if you're wrong? What if you die and found out the entire thing has been a cruel joke, or worse yet, there's . . . nothing?"

"Then there'd be nothing to know," I laughed. But I noticed Edward wasn't laughing. "Well, then, as C. S. Lewis put it, you would have paid the universe a compliment it doesn't deserve."

Edward leaned in very close and whispered into my ear, "You would pay me a compliment I don't deserve if you let me make love to you right here on this couch, right now."

I whispered back, "You would pay me a compliment I don't deserve if you let me keep your tattoo in my imagination."

Chuckling, Edward took my hand in a genial gesture instead. "How do you know there isn't nothing? I mean, after death, not when I take my pants down."

I have sparred with few sharper than Edward when it came to conflating spirituality with sexuality.

"Oh, I guess there are a million theological arguments on this side of heaven," I conceded. "But as for me, ultimately, I can't explain, I just *know.*"

"What?" Edward snapped.

"I *know,*" I snapped back.

"I mean, you know *what?*"

"I don't know, I just *know.*"

"That's such a cop-out," he responded flatly.

"Yeah, I know." I cringed at having to say the phrase yet again. "But it's true."

"Big gamble," he sighed.

"On the earthly playing field, yes, but on the spiritual one, no, I don't think so," I replied.

"Is that 'no' as in the negative, or 'know' as in 'you know for sure'?" he questioned.

"Very funny," I replied.

"I'm serious," he looked at me steadily.

"I know," I cringed as I said it again.

"It seems to me that Christianity is about a lot more 'no-ing' than 'knowing.' You have to say 'no' to everything fun, without even knowing why!" Edward flung himself into the far corner of the couch.

It occurred to me right then and there, although I couldn't put it into words, that the biblical "knowing" with sexual connotations also holds spiritual ones: the deep unity between a husband and a wife is indeed a reflection of God's relationship with each of us. We each long to be fully known. We each crave the privilege of growing to intimately know another. And when we experience it, we, well, *know*.

Edward got up and walked to the window. He studied the snow falling steadily outside.

"I don't see what you see," he sighed with resignation. "I don't *know*."

I wanted to say *Look! Look at what God has done for us! There is hope! There is knowing! We are indeed caught in a blizzard, with everything swirling around us, with nothing making any sense. We are utterly lost without this love. Seeing isn't always believing. But believing is always seeing, even in the swirling, even in the dark.*

But I didn't say a word. I didn't do anything. I just sat there. The sudden realization of why Jesus stood silent in front of the tribunal seared through me as the flames flickered out in the grate. At times, oh at so many times, what else is there to say? Just when the room seemed to grow its darkest, Edward turned slowly back toward me.

"But I am trying, Caro. Really, I'm trying."

I closed my eyes and handed my friend over to a hand I could not see but knew was there.

.ılıllıu.

Our schools teach our children about using protection when having sex. But what about being protected from sex, or through sex? Such complete intimacy of a covenant within a covenant helps protect a marriage; it fosters a powerful bond as well as a certain kind of shell around two people, enclosing them in the safety of each other within the safety of their God, shielding them from the blows of a fallen world, sustaining them to do good battle together, to run a good race together. No wonder *armor* and *amor* depend on the "are" of where you are at.

Sitting there studying Edward's silhouette against the wintered window, I also realized how obedience forms so many other layers of protection that we could never discern at the time of relying on faith. I could have really messed up things, not only for me but more significantly, even for him. True love for a friend, let alone a beloved, looks to nurture the other's faith walk as well. It seeks to protect. I had never really grasped what "protect" fully meant—of course when I heard the famous description of love from 1 Corinthians shared at wedding ceremonies, I thought of "protection" as running to save another from an immediate threat, or in laying down one's life for another. I hadn't thought of it as proactively trusting in obedience because of its impact on another as well.

It struck me how fragile Edward's own burgeoning faith was. And how I could have dealt it a blow, unintentionally, by having sex with him haphazardly, or even by flirting irresponsibly. As a believer, and therefore the one with more responsibility—and strength, and hopefully discernment—in the situation, how had my behavior been a "paean of praise to God"? As Sarah Young put it, in her imagining of Jesus' voice, "The more you focus on My Presence with you, the more fully you can enjoy life. Glorify Me through your pleasure in Me. Thus you proclaim My Presence to the watching world."

Contrary to how I automatically live my life, think my thoughts, or take action, it simply isn't all about me. Rick Warren was right to open his widely acclaimed book, *The Purpose Driven Life*, with exactly this premise. Only keeping our eyes on Jesus can help us steer that rudder out of the drowning depths of ourselves. Sometimes the navigation comes easy, but often I find it akin to trying to move a boulder away from a tomb. I cannot do it alone. And I cannot do it without groaning with the effort, with the despair, with the wordlessness of it at times. Romans 8:26-27 reminds us that the Spirit helps us in our weakness: "We do not know what we ought to pray for, but the Spirit himself intercedes for us through wordless groans. And he who searches our hearts knows the mind of the Spirit, because the Spirit intercedes for God's people in accordance with the will of God." We are not alone, not one of us: the main difference between a believer and a nonbeliever is that the believer knows it, or can be reminded of it, while a nonbeliever cannot. And the embodied word for the synapse of ever-presence remembered is Emmanuel.

Edward stood now with his back to the window, studying me in turn.

Thus you proclaim My Presence to the watching world.

"You like this son of a preacher man, don't you, Caro," he stated more than asked.

I was taken by surprise, but then again, I wasn't. I knew the Holy Spirit had brought thoughts of TDH to both of us at just such a time for just such a purpose. I spoke quietly but firmly, looking Edward straight in the eye.

"I think it would be safe to say that I don't know anyone quite like him."

Edward smiled broadly. "Me too."

We made some more coffee and talked about Edward's consideration of agnosticism, with a sort of "gentle leaning now—*perhaps*" as he put it, toward Christianity. The furnace repairman showed up just as we were making another pot. The two of us heard the doorbell clearly from the kitchen, and I rejoiced at not having missed the call. We offered him a cup after he finished the repair, and the three of us sat at the kitchen table together enjoying good company and the indoor thaw.

Shortly after the repairman left, Edward's friend arrived, honking outside. Bernie was anxious to get to a family gathering, especially as the snow had slowed him down, so he called out to Edward to gather his things. Edward put the jacket back on he had finally discarded when the house warmed up. While bending down to zip up his backpack, I heard him speak the words, "But I tell you that anyone who looks at a woman lustfully has already committed adultery with her in his heart."

"Did I just hear—?" I gasped. That sure was a different type of "line" altogether for Edward!

"Looks like I have a few things to work on yet," he cut me off as he stood up and winked.

"Hey!" I laughed. "You've been holding out on me. I didn't know you knew any Scripture!"

"Ah well, luv, just a few things here and there." Edward gave me a shy smile. But then he went into full Eddie mode; I could tell from the glint in those storm-gray eyes. "Mainly the ones about lust. Wasn't it you? Or maybe it was Theology Man? Anyway, one of you told me to start with what interests you, if nothing else. So I started with the Song of all Songs—isn't that what it's called? Wow, and with good reason too. Phew. Good read. Besides, everyone knows the sin parts, whether they own up to it or not."

"Ha, you've got me there!" I grinned.

He paused; his eyes grew dark and serious. "Truth be told, Caro, I have been dabbling in the Bible . . . you've had my curiosity piqued for some time. So has that crazy theology dude. And Evelyn and Andrew. And yeah, I guess Michael too, who, I have to admit, is a pretty likeable priest. You guys have something I want . . . something I can't quite put my finger on."

"It's hard to put into words, isn't it?" I said gently.

We smiled at each other.

"I know," I couldn't help saying as I hugged him. I wrapped an extra scarf around him and loaned him a toque—a proper Canadian hat against the cold—for good measure. "Stay warm and travel safely, you crazy Aussie."

"I'll give these back to you at school," he said responsibly. We both smiled at how this made us sound like children.

"No worries, mate," I said, in my best *Crocodile Dundee* accent.

The snow had finally stopped falling but the accumulation was immense. From the doorway, I watched Edward pause to see how he would navigate the un-shoveled drive to his friend's idling car. The world burned white behind him, strangely aglow even in the dark. It seemed literally a winter wonderland.

Father Wild (oh, that I should have such a name!) noted how "every snow crystal is hexagonal but within this basic six-sided shape there are endless intricate permutations and combinations so that virtually every flake is unique. What is the return on investment on such a colossal production? Is there some underlying beauty about reality that has to constantly manifest itself?" Anyone who has experienced the effect of a deep snowfall can tell you the marvel of how snow absorbs sound. Despite the busy city streets nearby, all was hushed. Indeed, all was calm, all was bright.

Edward finally stepped carefully down the icy driveway, singing out loudly as he slipped and shuffled. His voice rose all the clearer for the stillness around: "Nobody will know, when you're old, Caro, oh so old, that you was a beauty, a sweet sweet beauty. A sweet sweet beauty, but stone stone cold!"

I shook my head at him, at the juxtaposition of such blessedness and buffoonery. At the paradox of Edward. Of me. Of all of us. Of the Rolling Stones being part of a silent night. Of the serious joy of the holy fool! A paradox, however, is only a *seeming* contradiction, reconciled in grace by a faith we see by but cannot see. God, indeed, everywhere, and always. Both of us started laughing, and our laughter lifted to the heavens.

"See you on the other side of the pond, my sweet, sweet beauty," Edward called out as tipped his toque whilst bowing low.

Shivering but oddly warm, I was just about to step back in and close the door behind me when I heard Edward call out.

"Hey, Caro, look!"

There he stood, transfixed, outside the car, head tilted upward and steam rising from his open mouth. I followed his gaze to a blazingly full moon straight above us, awash in a night, as Byron put it so well, "of cloudless climes and starry skies." Vaulted by God's promise to Abraham, something settled deep within me as I, too, agape with *agape,* remained stilled within the white silence.

"When I see something like *that . . .*" Edward breathed.

Under and over the accumulation of such beauty, we gave each other a knowing look.

We have something of God within us the way we have something of the stars.

Chapter Five

ON THE ROAD

Boys and girls in America have such a sad time together;
sophistication demands that they submit to sex immediately
without proper preliminary talk. Not courting
talk— real straight talk about souls, for life
is holy and every moment is precious.

JACK KEROUAC

On a warm summer's evening in a 1974 Javelin bound for North Carolina, we were all too tired to sleep. So we rolled down the windows and stared into the darkness until the boredom overtook us, and Hannah began to speak.

"How much more Kenny Rogers can we possibly listen to?" she groaned as she stretched in her seat.

"I like Kenny Rogers," I replied.

"So do I," Mike chimed in. "A lot," he added menacingly when Hannah reached toward the cassette player of Mike's dad's favorite old car. This was the nineties, remember, so CDs were just coming out. TDH played them in his room, but he was a techie geek. He also had a laptop, one that was actually portable, unlike mine, which was akin to lugging around a sewing machine. I was home from Oxford for the long summer vacation, having navigated foreign territory for the last few years as a new Christian on the dating scene.

"Come on, *The Gambler*?" Vincent looked across at me with disgust. "What possible take-away value, let alone cultural edification, could there be in *that*?"

He took a small case from his front jacket pocket, flipped it open and peeled off a small, thin sheet of paper. From the other compartment in the case, he took a pinch of something and rolled it in the tissue. "Got a light?" he asked.

"How culturally edifying," I mumbled. Mike looked back at us through the rearview mirror, fixing his gaze on Vincent.

"In my car, you can smoke weed or you can make fun of Kenny Rogers, but you can't do both."

Vincent thought for a moment, then tucked his doobie back into his beautiful antique pocket case. The men locked eyes in the rearview mirror. The country and western gauntlet had been thrown, and now the heat in the car had reached high noon, mimicked eerily by the full moon outside. Hannah pulled herself up and I checked my seatbelt.

"Them lyrics are words to live by," Mike said in drawled defense of *The Gambler,* the ghost of whom seemed to be sitting with us, quieted by his mouthful of whiskey and riding shotgun. You could almost make out the burning ember of his cigarette. I squinted in the dark. I think the gambler-ghost had his arm around Mike's shoulder.

"Vince, you idiot, don't you dare light that up!" Hannah scolded over her shoulder. "You want us all to get arrested? We'll be crossing the border soon."

"That's exactly why I need it," Vincent replied calmly.

"Well, I know Americans are not as friendly as Canadians," I began, "but surely you don't need—"

"Very funny," Vincent cut me off. "I haven't been home for over three years, Carolyn. *Three years.*"

"I know you've been travelling abroad, Hannah told me, but surely you popped home for a Christmas here or a birthday there?" I asked.

"No."

"Why not?"

Vincent didn't answer. I knew it couldn't be due to financial restraint. Vincent came from old Southern money. He had been traveling since his graduation from Duke, staying at five-star resorts and private villas throughout Europe with friends and family connections. He wore Tretorn top to bottom and got his nails clipped and buffed. He jauntily kept his joints in an eighteenth-century porcelain snuff box that I would have locked behind glass, for goodness' sake. When he showed up at Oxford seeking to crash at Hannah's small flat, I wondered why he simply didn't take out a room at the grand Randolph, or at the very least one of the many quaint B & Bs. I wondered, that is, until Hannah explained their history: she and Vincent had dated when she was an exchange student during her undergraduate years in North Carolina. The whole event was a rather fast and furious affair, given the brevity of the academic program. Sparks flew and kindled with introductions at their theater arts class; the flame sputtered, however, after their final production when Hannah had to return to the United Kingdom. Vincent proclaimed undying love for her at the airport, flinging roses over the security checkpoint. Hannah sobbed all the way across the Atlantic. After several months had passed, however, across many letters promised but undelivered (absence speaks louder than presence), they both realized it wasn't to be, and with the discomfort lifted by the British pragmatism of the one only to be met by the Southern gentility of the other, both decided to become steadfast friends, staying in close touch ever since.

It was Hannah, the social hub of the entire universe, who had orchestrated this car trip. When she heard how TDH had offered us a friend's place to stay on our way through DC, she got in touch with Mike, a lifelong friend who had relocated to Toronto. Mike was still reeling from his father's recent death followed by his breakup with his longtime girlfriend. It was one of those life seasons for him when everything rains down at once and you find yourself drowning. Noah built the ark before the rains came, and for good reason. Mike wasn't for or against religion, and he held a gentle interest when he learned about my faith. But his anger at his father's untimely death ran fast and deep, and without anything else to hang on to, he found himself caught in its swirling undertow. Hannah thought it might do him good to come along with us on our trip, as he also had friends at her former college in Virginia, where he had visited her many times in the past.

"He could use a change of scenery," she said with her usual compassionate authority to a group of us at the pub one night shortly before we all left Oxford for the summer, "and besides, he *needs* an odyssey. The death of one's father demands it. Look at Telemachus, look at Jack Kerouac, look at Luke Skywalker, for crying out loud."

The rest of us solemnly agreed.

Once we were in Canada, Hannah contacted Vincent, who was on tour with a small British theater group in a town between Mike's family and mine. Their show run would be wrapping up about the time she arrived to visit me during the "long vac," as the Brits referred to summer vacation. She convinced Vincent to join us in my little London, Ontario, rather than return to the other big London. She told them that Mike had agreed to drive them all, knowing that

Vincent enjoyed meeting Mike in the past. Once Vincent showed up, she convinced him yet again to join us in our trek down South, claiming it really was time he went home. Mike told Vincent that he should seriously consider Hannah's point. It took a lot of coaxing and many a murmured conversation late into the night among the three of them after I'd gone to bed before Vincent finally relented to Hannah's plan. I have yet to meet anyone who could resist Hannah's persuasive powers for long. It may be due to her refreshing frankness or her airtight arguments coupled with a genuine care for your welfare, or her sheer persistence. Hannah could be like water on rock. Or, it simply may be the effect of her tossing that gorgeous red hair. Gingers do own superpowers the rest of us lack, after all.

"Well?" I prodded Vincent. He ignored my question and kept looking out the window into the night.

"You've got to know when to hold 'em . . ." sang Mike under his breath. Now it was Vincent's turn to glare at Mike.

"Caro," Hannah interrupted, "let's just say that tensions run a bit high at Vince's house." She turned in her seat and gave me *the look*. Usually Hannah is the first one to chat on and to encourage others to chat on with her, but *the look* translates into every language as: *shut up*.

But I went to open my mouth anyway. She raised her eyebrows and leaned in further, adding the silent but multilingual command: *now*. I sat back, mouth closed, defeated.

I peered at Vincent's profile, expecting him to still be ticked off at Mike, but he wasn't. Instead, he looked sad. He and Mike liked to wind each other up, and they could really bicker, but they also respected each other and held a mutual fondness for Hannah. For all of his usual urbane wit and self-composure, color-coordinated clothes, and cultured ease, Vincent now looked like a little boy afraid of something under his bed. I noticed he twisted his fingers anxiously in his lap. He kept stealing glances at Mike. I put my still hand over his fidgeting ones.

"You okay?" I asked.

"Yeah, just tired," he replied as he closed his eyes and rested his head back on the seat.

Mike moved his hand toward the console with another cassette in his hand.

"That had better be R.E.M.," Vincent muttered without opening his eyes.

"It's a mix I made of Canadian artists for the trip. You know, a little northern exposure for you Brits and Confederates." Mike winked at Hannah seated next to him.

"Don't force me to do drugs, Mike," Vincent growled next to me.

Mike laughed. "C'mon, it'll be fun to listen to."

It was hard to resist Mike, especially when he laughed, which, unfortunately, was rare in the wake of his father's death. With his mix of Iroquois, French, and Scottish heritage, he owned a chiseled profile, which I could admire to my heart's content undetected from the backseat (or so I thought, until I caught him catching me in the review mirror studying him, at which he gave me a devilishly disarming wink that reddened my cheeks through our entire ride across the tri-state area).

Fortunately, Gordon Lightfoot came on next, with his distinct folk charisma, drawing us all to sing with him. I looked back over at Vincent, the only one not singing. I noticed he was fiddling with another type of pill box I hadn't seen on him before. Studying Vincent, I continued to sing, "Sometimes I think it's a shame, when I get feeling better when I'm feeling no pain."

.ıllılılıı.

There are few things in life more painful than enduring unrequited love, and one of those is being trapped in a car on a long journey with someone in the throes of unrequited love. Or, make that, in the close company of multiple co-pilgrims suffering from such a fate. Or, make that, where *you* are the only one who isn't suffering at that particular moment acutely from unrequited love (or so you dare to hope), but everyone else within your reach is.

As we drove all those miles, I began to realize the dynamics of our little traveling world. Vincent was in love with Mike. Mike was in love with Hannah. Hannah was in love with Vincent. And me, well, I was in love with TDH, but would still be damned if I admitted to it. And at least *he* wasn't in the car with us. I would certainly have a lot to fill in for my good friend Abby once we arrived in DC. I could picture her curls bouncing along with her good humor. Abby had been my assigned mentor through my Bible study at St. Ebbe's back at Oxford. A more mature Christian, she met with me regularly for encouragement, accountability, and just general fun. And serious fun Abby was! She owned a huge heart for the Lord that was both joyous and searching. She left her native England to pursue mission studies in North Carolina, and a connection in her master's work had brought her into contact with TDH's current renowned pastor in DC. I had missed her company dearly over the vacation and now greatly anticipated a good long-into-the-night catch-up with her. Although, with her personal motto of courtesy and frankness, I knew she would be deftly curious about my "visit" with TDH.

As we listened to Alanis Morissette, Vincent explained how he hadn't seen his parents since they blew up over his last visit when he tried to talk with them about his being gay. Mike talked about how he couldn't blame Vincent's parents. Hannah shared how painful it is to not only have someone leave you, but to have someone leave you for someone of the same sex. I didn't say anything to anyone; it was all, indeed, a jagged little pill to swallow.

It was a hot and muggy day when we pulled up at the address TDH had emailed me where he was now living in Washington, DC. We had the air conditioning on full blast in the car but it had barely made a dent in the humidity. The place was a beautiful brownstone situated only a few blocks from the Capitol.

"Wow." Hannah nudged me. "Looks like Theology Man has done well for himself!"

"He shares it with four other guys, Hannah." I nudged her back.

"Well, regardless," Mike observed admiringly, "it's a pretty cool spot. Do you want us to wait until you're in safely?"

"Thanks, but no, you guys go ahead," I replied. I knew Hannah was eager to make it to her UVA friends' dinner party, and they still had some distance to go in the growing afternoon traffic. "He told me where they leave a spare key if no one's home to let me in. I'll be fine."

"Okay, then." Mike waved along with the others as I got out of the car with my small bag. I had forced myself to pack only one other outfit so that I wouldn't appear too high maintenance. Hannah had scoffed when she saw it. "I'll accessorize." I smiled sweetly at her.

"We'll be back for you tomorrow then, around the same time," Mike confirmed.

"Sounds good," I leaned into the car window to give Hannah one last hug.

"You're nervous!" she whispered in my ear.

"No," I lied.

"Yes, you're shaking like a leaf." She looked right at me.

I had to admit, my palms were sweaty, too, and I felt a little light-headed. I hadn't seen TDH in over a year, since his last visit to England when we had dinner as friends. I pulled myself up straight and took a deep breath. The air about me felt close and steamy; for a moment I thought I heard thunder roll in the background . . . or was that just the traffic?

"Godspeed!" Hannah called out of the window, laughing. They honked as they pulled away, leaving me standing alone on the sidewalk. Before I could lose my confidence, I turned and walked up the front steps and rang the doorbell. No answer. I used the knocker. Still no answer. I waited what I thought to be the decorous amount of time. *Surely with five guys living here, someone must be home?* I muttered to myself. But several minutes and repeated knocks later, still no one came to the door. I looked at my watch. It wasn't yet 5 p.m.; most likely they were all still at their various intern positions. Perhaps one of them would walk up? I did feel a little awkward about letting myself in. So I sat down on the step, reasoning it wouldn't hurt to wait just a little longer.

That's when I felt the first one.

Kerr-plop. A big drop of rain. Not the gentle kind that gives you lots of courteous warning, but the heavy type that forebodes an onslaught in about three . . . two . . . one . . .

The sky cracked open and down came the drops in torrents. I sprinted down the main steps and took a sharp turn onto the basement stairwell, which ran down the porch on the opposite side leading to a small, plain door in a lower space not much larger than a window well. The key, I had been told, would be hidden under the mat here. But there was no mat. There was no key. There was nothing. Not a brick, nor a plant, nor even a ceramic frog. Nothing in the shallow lower doorway except, I noticed forlornly, mounds of debris clogging the small drain.

The rain began coming down even harder, if that was at all possible. Water streamed over my face and matted my hair to my forehead and neck. My thin skirt stuck to my legs and I immediately regretted wearing a white T-shirt.

With the drain clogged, the water began to rise around my ankles, soaking my sandals and then rising up to my calves. I bent down, elbow deep in murky runoff, feeling around for anything resembling a key along the edge of the step I could no longer see.

As thunder crashed and lightening flashed, I heard someone calling out to me from above—a beautiful voice, like how I would imagine a Michelangelo sculpture to sound, if it could speak. I stopped my searching, and stood there, like the escape scene from *The Shawshank Redemption*. Parting my limp, wet locks from my dirt-spattered face, I squinted up into the downpour. Blinking, I tried to get a clear look at the vision above me.

It was Robert Redford! *The Natural* was staring down at me from the railing above, leaning over with a concerned look on his face. In disbelief, I blinked again.

"Miss, are you okay?" The Beautiful Voice asked.

I couldn't say anything in response. I was struck dumb at the prospect of Robert Redford talking to me from a stairwell in a storm.

"Miss? What are you up to?" the Robert God asked with increasing concern. The storm raged up behind him. Forks of lightening haloed his head. *Sundown, you better take care, if I find you been creeping 'round my back stairs.*

My own voice finally came out a squeak, like the drowned rat I literally had become.

"I was told there was a key here," I stammered. I felt my face go so hot I was sure it was steaming in the rain. "I'm sorry, but when no one came to the door and then it started to storm, I thought I better let myself in and so I . . ." my voice trailed off. Robert, I noticed, wore a quizzical look on his face. He was probably wondering how best to sneak away and call the cops. I stood there, hapless. Debris circled in the water up to my knees now.

"Oh, you must be *Caro!*" he finally shouted over the rain. I felt my face go even hotter, as if that, too, were possible. How did Robert Redford know my name?

He quickly came down the steps and extended his hand to me, in the most gallant of ways. I had no choice but to take it, since I had to suction myself out of the mire; the rain was coming so hard and fast, I could barely see. He led me up the stairs and into the grand foyer of the majestic turn-of-the-century house. We were both soaked to the skin. As I stood there dripping and creating a puddle on the marble floor, the gorgeous Sundance kid grabbed a couple towels from the nearby bathroom and handed me one.

"Hi, I'm Brad," he said warmly, while drying himself off.

"Hi," I said, a bit disappointedly since realizing as I wiped my eyes clear that he was not, in fact, a young Robert Redford, though the resemblance was uncanny.

"We were expecting you," Brad continued. "But I feel badly that the key wasn't there. We moved it a couple days ago since there had been a lot of break-ins in the area lately."

"That's okay, of course," I tried smiling, but instead I was now shivering in the air conditioning.

"He won't be home for some time yet, I'm afraid. He called earlier to say he'd be stuck at a function later than planned but that he'd hurry back, and to tell you to wait if you beat him here, and . . ." Brad gave me a big grin, "that he'd like to take you for dinner."

"Oh, I see." I turned to pick up my bag, which was much heavier now sopping wet. The material, I noticed with dismay, was soaked through: so much for a backup outfit.

"I don't want to put anyone out. I'll just find a place to have a coffee and pop back later."

Brad intercepted, taking the bag from me and starting up the dark wood staircase.

"Nonsense. It's awful out there, and you are welcome to stay here. You need a warm shower. And a change of clothes."

I seemed unable to move.

"Come on," he called out over his shoulder.

Slowly, I followed him up the sweep of the stunning stairway, gawking at the floorplan below.

"This place is huge!" I gasped.

"Yeah, it's a fun spot," Brad replied. "Our church owns it, along with the house next door. The guys stay in this one, the women in the other. It provides an affordable place to stay for us postgrads while we make our way in the big, scary political world."

"Good plan," I replied, laughing. Somehow, I had imagined TDH stuck in a hovel with men in stained shirts eating ramen noodles. These Christians, I had to admit, were connected. Brad walked to the end of the upstairs hall. He opened the last door wide and stepped aside for me to enter.

"Here's his room. He has his own bathroom to the right. Feel free to shower and change in there. He won't be back for a few hours yet."

I stepped hesitantly inside. I felt a bit awkward about going into TDH's room without his knowledge. But then, I had to admit, curiosity trumped awkwardness. So did messy hair. I was grateful for the opportunity to redo my hair and touch up my makeup before seeing him again for the first time in ages. How quickly had I become Southern on this trip! As Brad turned to leave, I called him back.

"Um, I'm sorry about this . . . but I'm afraid I don't have anything to change into."

We both looked at the soaked bag he had set down by the door. In the meantime, I myself was still dripping so badly that a ring of water had already collected around me.

"Oh, right. I see. I can put your clothes in the dryer?" he offered. "But it may be some time for them to dry. It hasn't been working at full capacity—we keep meaning to get it fixed." He gave me an apologetic look as he passed me another towel. I raised my eyes, assuming this was not only to dry me with after the shower, but then to wear for some time after as well. Brad must have read my look but without saying anything else, he glanced around. Then he strode over to a dresser, pulling out some clothes.

"Here!" He tossed me a striped rugby shirt and pair of sweats. Both were huge. I opened my mouth to complain, but then realized my options, under the circumstances, were somewhat limited.

"Thank you," I said instead.

"If you'd like, I can come back in half an hour and give you a tour of the house?" Robert, I mean Brad, offered.

"That sounds lovely."

"I'll knock loudly," he grinned big again.

"Sounds good." I smiled back thankfully.

The hot shower felt great after being drenched to the bone. I towel-dried my hair and twisted it up in a somewhat (I hoped) more attractive knot than the previous mess it had been. Then I reapplied a little makeup for good measure and breathed a sigh of relief and thanks. It's the little graces in life that really count.

I put on TDH's clothes, pulling the drawstrings on the sweats as tight as I could around my waist. Everything hung off of me, but I had to admit, his shirt smelled wonderful.

Now that I was comfortable and dry, and looking a little less worse for wear, I tried to decide how best to occupy myself until TDH got home. I certainly didn't want to venture out of the room dressed like I was, in case I ran into someone other than Brad. So I figured I would explore TDH's room a little—just a little—until Brad came back.

The room was recent graduate student sparse, consisting of only a mattress on the floor, a desk, and an old recliner that tipped back dangerously when I tried sitting down. After almost tumbling onto the floor, I decided it was best to remain standing, so I walked over to his bookshelf. It teamed with theology books. Several photos decorated his wall, mainly of family and friends, and a few of him with girls whom I did not recognize. I peered at those ones especially closely. A loud knock at the door startled me.

"Yes?" I called out.

"It's me, Brad," I heard the familiar kind voice through the door. "All decent?"

"Yes," I tried to sound nonchalant. "Please come in."

Brad entered with a cup of steaming coffee and my dry clothes.

"That didn't take too long after all!" I said, gratefully sipping the delicious drink. It was strong and exactly how I liked it—just what I needed, I thought, to brace for me for the evening ahead.

"Somehow, miraculously, the dryer was hotter than usual," Brad winked.

I took my clothes and changed in the bathroom. Then I followed Brad out onto the landing for a tour of the gorgeous old home. I love architectural history, and Washington, DC, certainly had that aplenty. The homes on this street were no exception, and it was fascinating to see the old wrought-iron elevators, the formal dining rooms, and the attention to detail and craftsmanship. Two of the other housemates came home while I waited for TDH. I met them and was charmed by their conversation. After changing, they excused themselves to attend a black-tie dinner. It would seem that the social calendar in DC during a Congressional session ran somewhat akin to that of Oxford during term.

"I'm not sure what's holding him up." Brad looked at his watch once we finally ended back upstairs. "I feel like a terrible host." He looked at me anxiously. "But I have to be at an event myself here shortly. If he runs any later, I can certainly delay until I know you are in good hands."

I thanked Brad for his graciousness but assured him I would be just fine waiting for TDH in his room.

"I brought something to read," I told him. "And if it's still too damp, I'm sure he has something to read."

"That he does," Brad smiled warmly.

We said our goodbyes and I nestled carefully into TDH's chair that tipped precariously, making sure I steadied it against the wall. It was either that or his mattress on the floor, and I thought stretching out on the latter might be a bit presumptuous.

I was lost in some Alister McGrath book from his shelf, which I noticed had been signed, when I heard steady, confident footsteps coming up the stairs. I held my breath: slowly the doorknob turned, and in less than a moment, after a long time apart, TDH's familiar form filled the doorframe. We both stared at each other, neither of us moving or saying a word.

Finally, he came rushing toward me, pulling me out of the chair and on to my feet.

"Caro!" he exclaimed warmly. "How wonderful to see you!"

I tried to detect any reservation, judgment, cynicism, inconvenience . . . but the words merely rang of sincerity. Complete TDH sincerity. I hugged him before I could stop myself. He held me close and laughed. A deep, resonating laugh. Then he checked himself and pulled away.

"I apologize for being late—I knew you were set to arrive just before dinner but I couldn't get away from my new boss. I ran all the way here!" Indeed, he looked like he had. He was flushed, with specks of rain on his shirt.

"How was your trip? How are you enjoying the States? How is the doctorate going? How is Oxford treating you?" The questions tumbled out of him breathlessly, and I, breathless in return, didn't know how or where to begin. He laughed again as I pulled back and he looked me steady in the eye. "I'm sorry, so sorry. It's just so good to see you! How are *you*?"

Any worry I had about coming to visit instantly evaporated along with the rain as I enjoyed being enveloped in his warm presence again. He swept me downstairs and out the door, where we walked to a nearby restaurant and enjoyed a long, lingering dinner over good food and good conversation. After he paid the bill (he insisted, and I knew better than to argue on that one by now), we strolled back toward the Capitol under the stars, talking the entire time. Then he walked me to the house next door to his, the one where the female Christian students lodged and where he had arranged for me to stay. After introductions and more coffee with my hostesses in the equally elegant living room, they showed me to the room I was to use that belonged to one of the interns who was away. They all fussed over me and, in good humor, had me say things like "about" over and over again in my Canadian accent.

"It's almost as cute as Abby's," one of them commented. Abby, who was my dear, dear friend from Bible study at Oxford, was staying here too, and I would have the chance to see her tomorrow. What a small world indeed is this one in God's hands! It was obvious that this houseful of women were whip smart: all of them were highly educated, independent, and yet compassionate in their faith and generous in their hospitality. Finally assured that I was very comfortable indeed in the extra room, my new girlfriends went off to bed as I lingered over saying goodbye to TDH at the side door connecting to the lane between the two houses.

In the glow of the streetlamp pouring in and the soft summer air caressing our faces with all the sweetness following a storm, I waited with bated breath as he leaned in closer. Closing my eyes, I felt him kiss my cheek, as soft as the night breeze itself. Then he bid me goodnight. I watched him step lightheartedly down the steps and across the lane, whistling. Once on his porch, he gave me a little wave.

"Sleep well!" he called out. "I'll be by early to pick you up!"

"Where are we going?" I managed to call back, still somehow breathless, and irritated at myself for being so.

"You'll see," he winked. Then he was gone.

Needless to say, I did not sleep well. But oh, how I dreamed . . .

.ı‖‖ıı.

The next day, TDH and I enjoyed a beautiful day together. We toured DC, we talked, and we ate lunch at a wonderful restaurant after strolling the quaint streets of Georgetown. We talked. We enjoyed dinner back at his place with his housemates. We talked. Finally, when everyone else had gone up to bed, we sat close to each other on the couch in the wainscoted front room. We talked. And then, we were quiet. All was quiet. TDH took my hand.

It had been like old times between us, so easy to talk and so easy, as well, to be silent together. And yet it was like new times now, too, for there was no cynicism or judgment nor anything to prove from me. Rather, our shared faith rolled in between us, along with the realization of how much we admired each other, and how much we enjoyed each other's company, and how much, well, we had *missed* each other. With all the soul talking, there was also that spark, or that sparkling, between us, that only grew more noticeable in the hushed dark (as sparks tend to do).

We sat *thisclose* together on the couch. I dared not move, let alone breathe. The electricity crackled between us. I could smell his familiar and distinct scent, reminiscent from our Oxford days; my heart began beating like a big brass band. I thought for certain he would lean in and kiss me as he held my hand tight. But, alas, he did not. Instead he reached over and tucked a loose piece of my hair behind my ear, in the most tender of ways. He looked deep into my eyes, and then broke the silence by whispering it was time to say goodnight. Jolted out of reverie, I suddenly realized just how late it was. Where had the time, as always with him, gone? I admired his restraint and his treatment of me. But I also wanted to scream: "I leave tomorrow morning! What about us?" I thought about kissing him instead, but something held me back, something stronger than just female decorum or even pride. Somehow, in some way, I knew that a kiss would be a match to a flame, and that flame to a bonfire, and that it would not just be playing with fire, we would be fire . . . all consumed and all consuming . . . and that this antique couch was in fact holy ground, on which even angels fear to tread, with good reason.

As Grace Irwin put so well in *Least of all Saints*, "It's a question of denying ourselves immediate pleasure in order to reap a keener pleasure later on." Delayed gratification instills deeper appreciation and enjoyment in pretty much every experience I could think of. Why would sex be any different? Why would heaven be so either? What if our bodies and relationships in this fallen life were indeed the templates for our resurrected life? "For as, when the spirit serves the flesh, it is fitly called carnal," observed Augustine, "so, when the flesh serves the spirit, it will justly be called spiritual."

Reluctantly, I bid TDH goodnight as well, and headed next door to join the women at the neighboring house. The next morning I woke very early, when the city still slept and the sunrise barely blushed the horizon beyond the Capitol. I rolled back over and tried closing my eyes, but I couldn't sleep any longer, I knew. In only a few short hours I would be leaving DC. My friends would be circling back in the Javelin to pick me up on the final leg of our trip. I got up and crept quietly down the stairs, trying to avoid making any of the old floorboards creak so as to not wake my kind hostesses.

When I reached the bottom of the stairs and turned to enter the kitchen, I was surprised to see the patio door open and a figure curled up on the chaise lounge. A head of bouncy golden curls pored over a book open on her lap. It took me only a moment to recognize those curls—it was Abby, sipping coffee and reading so intently she didn't even notice me standing there. I didn't want to startle her, so I cleared my throat.

I was first introduced to Abby through mutual Christian friends at Oxford. We ended up attending St. Ebbe's Church together and often went for long walks together after service in Port Meadows. Vivacious, wickedly funny, and smart, I always enjoyed Abby's company. She also loved God with genuine and contagious delight, and welcomed authentic conversation about faith questions big and small. In turn, I was delighted to discover that not only would she be in DC at the same time as my visit, but also that, in fact, she would be staying next door to TDH as a guest in the women's house since she would be there doing research for her thesis work. Little did I know that soon after our time together in DC, she would be engaged to TDH's housemate Robert, er, I mean Brad—but that's another book.

That morning, I interrupted Abby reading her devotionals. She shared with me how she loved this private time, how she rose early every morning to bask in her quiet time with God. Categorically, I had previously been wary of folks who claim to read their Bible at the break of day. I had long been nocturnal by nature and took Jesus' invitation to "Come to me, . . . and I will give you rest" as justification for pulling the covers over my head after hitting the snooze button for the third time. Abby, however, was so earnest, so winsome, so completely in love with Jesus and going to him first that it was hard not to take her seriously. Obviously, that's how she took God. So much so that she didn't do anything else in her day until she had taken him at his word and taken in his Word.

"How was your time with TDH yesterday?" she asked in usual Abby fashion—that is, not wasting any time with small talk.

Abby knew I cared for TDH; she had watched our relationship tentatively grow over the years and the miles. She had watched my relationship with Jesus develop as well.

"It was fabulous," I couldn't help smiling.

"So glad, luv," she smiled back. "But of course, we knew it would be."

"It's amazing," I marveled. "Whenever I see him, I am reminded of just how special he is. He is unlike anyone else I know."

"I know others like him," she smiled again.

"True. But I didn't know men like him existed, if I'm honest."

"In what way?" she asked.

"These Christian men, I mean these men who really seek to know and follow Christ, they are, well, so *different*. So unlike other men."

"I'd agree. Just like we should be unlike 'other' women. I would hope that followers of Christ would seem 'different,' as you put it," Abby said simply.

"In the best sense, in the most loving sense," I felt my way through the clarification, "I guess that is what TDH is to me." I couldn't help giggling, but I also meant it fervently, "A kind of Superman, a hero, a—"

"Savior?" Abby interrupted.

"No . . . well . . ." suddenly I felt a bit shaky. "*No,*" I emphasized more confidently.

She raised her brows then closed her devotional, setting it aside.

"What is the desire of your heart, Caro?" she asked gently.

"What?" I echoed uncertainly.

"Exactly. *What*?" She looked right at me.

"What *what*?" I always stall when caught off guard, like a vintage Jaguar in unexpected inclement weather. Or, perhaps more in my case, like an old Chevy.

"What is the desire of your heart, in terms of your relationship with God?" Abby kept her foot on the gas pedal and turned the key in the ignition.

"Well, to know God better." I was trying not to flood.

"Hmm." Abby didn't say anything else.

"I'm serious," I replied with enough indignance, I hope, to mask the unease at being caught in my own lack of conviction.

"I am too," Abby persisted. "And you, my dear, are seriously nutters. Who actually says that kind of thing?"

"You would. You're a committed Christian." There, I thought. That should get her off my case.

"Committed, like dedicated? Or committed, like to an asylum?" Abby shook her glorious curls.

"Very funny," I said, as flatly as my own hair.

"You will need to be more specific. No rote answers, luv." Abby wouldn't let it go.

Man, just when I thought I was free of the Brits and could hide behind my comforting jargon, here pops one out of the American woodwork, with her bloodhound nose for detecting BS, especially of the spiritual sort.

"Okay . . ." I sighed. "Since you won't let it go . . ."

"*I won't?*" Abby tucked her legs in under her on the comfy chair. I knew that sign from her. It meant she was hunkering in for a good talk. There was no hiding now.

"I'm not the one refusing to let 'it' go here."

"What's the 'it'?" I asked, but in the asking, I had the answer. I had to admit, I was having trouble letting my "it" go. With complete sincerity, Abby reached over and took my hand.

"Ok, then, Caro, what is the desire of your heart, in terms of your relationship with TDH?" She pulled a chair closer to her with her toe, and then invited me to sit. My jaw dropped as I sat.

"What?" I finally managed a squeak of insult.

"You heard me." She didn't miss a beat.

"He completes me," I said with all the deadpan seriousness I could muster.

"Oh. My. Gawd." Abby virtually gagging.

"Okay, okay, bad I know," I shrugged.

"Yes, yes, very. No more of that Tom Cruise nonsense," she warned me in her clipped British accent.

"Okay then . . . he is in a category all his own. Not Cruise, TDH," I clarified.

"On a pedestal all his own too?" She studied me keenly.

"No, of course not," I retaliated.

"What is it you expect of him?"

"What do you mean?"

"If you were to marry, what would you expect of him?"

"Isn't that quite a leap, *Abby*?"

"Don't you think for one minute that I don't think that you haven't thought about it, *Caro*." Abby gave me the kind of look that made me feel as though I had been caught writing TDH's last name after my first name in big goofy cursive a hundred times in my school notebook.

Which I had, kinda, in a way, just on a few sticky notes . . . but I digress . . .

"Well," I began hesitantly. "*If* we were to get married, which we won't, because I never plan on marrying, and, of course, he might have other plans . . ."

"Of course. But *if* . . ."

"Then I guess I would expect him to love me unconditionally, not cheat on me, support me, know what I need . . ."

"Go on."

"Be a provider. Be a good father. Be, well, good in bed."

We laughed. Then Abby prompted me again, "Go on."

"Well, he should be able to make wise decisions, lead our family, help us grow in Christ, model what it means to have a thoughtful faith . . ."

"I see. And?" Abby asked.

"You want more?"

"You have more, don't you?" Again, she looked at me keenly.

"I guess I want him to take care of me but not smother me. Help me but not bulldoze me. I want him to respect my intellectual pursuits and my career and yet provide enough financial and emotional stability to give me the freedom to be solely a mother, should I choose, or change professional paths, if I'd like."

"Hmm," Abby interjected as I stopped for breath. "What about looks?"

"What about them? I'm not *that* shallow," I admonished her.

"None of us is *that* deep, Caro. What if he doesn't shower as often as you like? Or gets out of shape?"

"Okay, I guess there is a basic modicum of personal hygiene I should be able to expect. But I don't really care what his weight is, or how he dresses, or whether he grows or cuts his hair."

"Lucky guy." She took a sip of her coffee.

"Are you being facetious?" I asked.

"Me? Never. I'm just relieved, because it sounds like a pretty tall order as it is."

"He *is* pretty tall."

"You know what I mean."

"No I don't, actually," I decided to retaliate. "What's wrong if I have a few expectations?"

"A *few*? Caro, you have an army of them. And all prepared for battle!" Abby set her mug down with a thud. "And those are only the ones you'll admit to. I bet you have a bunch more you will assume he should know about without you having to speak them!"

"Shouldn't a girl have standards, spoken or unspoken?" I pulled myself up. "Besides, I would think he would like being the center of my world. Receiving my confidence and being admired? Isn't that what Christian guys in particular want? Adoration and importance? Aren't we called as wives to honor and respect our husbands? And besides, he is, truly, a great guy."

"A man," Abby stated.

"Okay, a man," I replied, irritated. "You are so, well, *British* to correct my slang like that."

"Don't end with a determiner," Abby scolded.

"What?" I realized I had said "what" a lot in this conversation. Maybe, I realized with a shot of humility, I needed some correction after all.

"Never mind," Abby continued. "Look, what I mean is that TDH is a man. And only a man."

"I know *that*."

"No, I don't think you do," she said quietly.

"What do you mean?" Now it was my turn to look at her keenly.

"I mean," Abby took a breath then went on, "that you are poisoning the well before you even drink from it. Or, perhaps more aptly, all the 'well' in this fallen world is tainted. You both may be well intentioned, and such intentions may even come from genuine admiration for genuinely admirable qualities, but the point is, he is still a man. And you, my dear, are a woman of God first and foremost."

Abby got up and poured me a cup of coffee as I sat there in stunned disbelief at what I had been doing. I had no words for what swirled in my head. Slowly, I sipped my steaming coffee, grateful that Abby had remembered with perfection how I liked it.

Swallowing in silence seemed the most appropriate language for the moment. After all, I had been breaking the first commandment. With the best of intentions, mind you, but even our best falls short of the mark. And the consequences of such fallen brokenness involve collateral damage. Not only was I placing something, or perhaps even worse, someone, ahead of God in my life, I was hurting the person I thought I was loving most in doing so. The expectations were crushing! And a recipe for disaster—both for him, and for me. We must, indeed, learn how to order our loves. The commandments are in their particular order for good reason: for God's reason. To use Hannah Whitall Smith's timeless reminder, "As usual, we put feeling first, and faith second, and the fact last of all, whereas God's invariable rule in everything is, fact first, faith second, and feeling last of all, the fact on which all else is predicated being that when you give yourself to God, He accepts you, and at once let your faith take hold of this fact. Then your feeling will follow." In other words, I was starting to fully realize, only one man was perfect, *is* perfect, and that man was also equally God.

Abby sat back down across from me.

"Oh man," I finally groaned.

"Precisely," Abby nodded, then passed me her well-worn copy of Oswald Chambers.

.ıllıllıı.

My friends returned to pick me up later that morning. As we pulled away, TDH stood on the sidewalk and waved. I kept thinking...kept hoping...that he would run after the car like the eponymous Harry ran for Sally in the film's New Year's Eve finale. But he didn't. I slumped back in the seat as the car rounded the bend toward Virginia.

St. Augustine wrote:

> And therefore it is that humility is specially recommended to the city of God as it sojourns in this world, and is specially exhibited in the city of God, and in the person of Christ its King; while the contrary vice of pride, according to the testimony of the sacred Writings, specially rules his adversary the devil. And certainly this is the great difference which distinguishes the two cities of which we speak, the one being the society of the godly men, the other of the ungodly, each associated with the angel that adhere to their party, and the one guided and fashioned by love of self, the other by love of God.

What a trip between the two cities, from the love of pride to the pride of love!

"Where love is, God is," Henry Drummond beautifully reminded us, "He that dwelleth in love dwelleth in God. God is love. Therefore *love*. Without distinction, without calculation, without procrastination, love. Lavish it upon the poor, where it is very easy; especially upon the rich, who often need it most; most of all upon our equals, where it is very difficult, and for whom perhaps we each do least of all." And to expect nothing in return, not one drop, but to love for the sake of loving—that is what God embodies and models to us all.

We listened to the Crash Test Dummies as we drove around the UVA campus.

"I think TDH looks just like Clark Kent, especially with those cute theology reading glasses," Hannah remarked.

"Clark Kent, now there was a real gent," Mike crooned with a sly grin.

"Is he the strong, silent type?" Vincent asked me. "You know—the 'still waters run deep' kind?"

I gave it some thought.

"I guess you could say so."

Vincent sighed.

"He doesn't talk a whole lot," Hannah interrupted. "But when he does, I don't know, it's like people really listen. Maybe because he doesn't talk a whole lot—unlike with people who do talk a lot. They can be easier to tune out."

"Hm? Were you saying something?" Mike responded absent-mindedly. Hannah reached across and poked him hard in the ribs.

"Hey! Careful! You almost made me go off the road!" Mike yelped back.

Off the road . . . that was me. In the words of Dante's famous beginning to *The Divine Comedy*: "In the middle of the journey of our life, I came to myself, in a dark wood, where the direct way was lost."

Leaving my world to visit TDH in his had been a risk. What if I had been wrong about the spark I thought we both felt? What if I was an idiot for leaving home to visit a guy I had known in what seemed now like almost a lifetime ago? Or worse, what if I really had inadvertently replaced Jesus with TDH?

What if I was stuck between the two cities?

"Sometimes I despair the world will never see another man like him," I sang the refrain quietly.

Then I realized I had to ask myself again—I had to remind myself and reorder my loves: which "him" was in my hymn?

Crash Test Dummies. I felt like one for sure.

.₁₁₁₁₁₁₁₁₁.

As we pulled over to get gas, Mike turned off the ignition and suddenly asked me what I thought of sexual orientation as a Christian.

"Well, what would Jesus say?" he prompted. "Should we kick Vincent to the curb?"

Although he said it with a smirk, I couldn't quite tell if Mike was joking or not. I took a deep breath.

"Jesus doesn't respond to anyone—well, except the judgmental Pharisees perhaps—with 'you stink.'" I opened the car door, stepped out, and then leaned back in Mike's window, adding, "Although he had every right to say it to any and all of us."

Hannah laughed.

"Anyone want a coffee?" I asked. "I'm going in to get one of those fancy ones, from the machine. My treat?"

"You mean the cheap ones." Hannah laughed again.

"Sure," Vincent said vaguely.

Mike said nothing but got out on his side and began pumping gas.

When I reached in my purse at the cash register, I realized that someone had hidden inside an envelope with my name on it. I recognized the distinct handwriting at once. Prickling with excitement, I tore it open right there. At first I thought it was empty, but then a very small slip of paper caught my eye. Inside, on a sticky note, was a single mark of punctuation:

?

I smiled to myself as I returned with gas station coffees. With us and the car refueled, we kept on truckin' . . . riding in the same car together toward the same destination but with faith in the end as well as the means making all the difference. E. M. Forster wrote, "Death destroys a man, but the idea of death saves him." Our idea of death converts what our idea of life—no matter how short, long, or unborn—means as well. "Life is always fatal," as Peter Kreeft puts it so well. But love is not. Love is stronger than death.

We listened in silence to the Grateful Dead, one of the few American rock bands we all conceded to listen to on our epic Canadian journey. Then, as though in response to Kenny Rogers, Mike looked at Vincent in the rearview mirror and sang along, "like the do-dah man once told me, 'You've got to play your hand.'"

Vincent joined in, "Sometimes the cards ain't worth a dime, if you don't lay 'em down."

"You need to forgive your folks, Vince," Mike spoke gently. "Especially your dad."

"Yeah, I know," Vincent replied.

We drove in silence for a while. The CD had stopped playing but no one reached to play the next song.

"Sometimes I miss my dad so much it physically hurts," Mike finally said, his words catching in his throat.

"So do I," Vincent replied quietly.

.ıılllıı.

After a little while of driving in more silence, Vincent pointed ahead to a picturesque country lane winding up a treed hilltop.

"This is the way home," he told us. As we approached, the columns of a beautiful Southern mansion peeked white out of the thick green. "Y'all are welcome to stay with us, as I've said from the start." I noticed that Vincent's drawl became more pronounced the further south we drove. "But now knowing what you do, I won't hold it against any of you if it's just easier to drop me off and then head to the hotel in town."

"What?" I exclaimed as we turned into the lane, the gravel crackling under our tires announcing our arrival. "And miss staying in this place?!"

"Wow," Hannah whistled low. "It looks like something straight out of *Gone with the Wind!*"

We pulled up just as the front door opened. A golden retriever bounded toward the car to greet us, then two elderly faces peered out, expectantly.

"I'm coming in with you." Hannah put her hand on Vince's shoulder.

"Yeah," Mike corrected Hannah as he swung his door open, "*we* are." As the rest of us held our breath, the two men held each other's looks. Then they suddenly smiled genuinely at each other.

Marveling, I got out of the car to stretch, reaching my arms up to the darkling sky. The question mark burned in my hand. *Sometimes the light's all shinin' on me; other times, I can barely see. Lately, it occurs to me, what a long, strange trip it's been.*

Chapter Six

GUEST NIGHT

Grant me chastity and continence, but not yet.

St. Augustine

I studied my reflection in the Top-
shop change-room mirror. Linnea,
my dear and most fashionable of friends, stood next to me, hugging
herself with delight.

"Oh, Caro!" she squealed. "It's dynamite! *You,* my love, are dy-no-mite!"

I had to admit: the dress packed quite a punch. On one hand, it
was every woman's dependable go-to outfit for a special occasion: an
LBD or "little black dress." Except that this one, while very black, was
not quite so little. The skirt swept almost to the floor, and with long
sleeves and a closed neckline, it appeared sleekly conservative from
the front. I loved the cut of the silhouette and the simple lines, un-
derstatedly elegant. But when you turned around—*kaboom!* The
back was almost completely yet tastefully cut out, revealing bare
shoulders and inviting the braille of the spine to be read by an encir-
cling hand. The playful dress made one look like a nun from the front
and a fifties movie star from the back. I had never worn anything so
daring! I wasn't sure I had the nerve.

"And it's on *sale!*" Linnea clapped her hands with glee.

I guess that was the tipping point for me in deciding to make my purchase. Shopping is the female equivalent of hunting and gathering. A woman feels no less triumphant after a good "kill"—perhaps even more so, after nailing a good deal! I could purchase this weapon of a dress and *still* afford to eat for the rest of the month on my scholarship allowance.

Abby arrived at the store to join us for lunch. She gave me a gape-mouthed look over as I tried the dress on one more time and turned around for her, too, under Linnea's beaming approval. Abby gave a low whistle.

"Wow, girl," she proclaimed. "Now there's a real saint-sinner outfit."

I winked at her over a half-black, half-bare shoulder. Women are the pinnacle of creation with good reason, after all.

.ılıllıılı.

This dress was for *me*. For glorious, singular, fully-in-love-with-Jesus-first me. And, if I'm honest, I was perhaps a bit relieved to love only Jesus first because any other intimate relationship seemed irrelevant to me back then. I was planning to wear this killer dress for a very special occasion that I would be attending, quite purposely, without a romantic date. My guest was going to be my friend Linnea, who always was up for a fashionable bash and could be counted on for a good time.

But, as the old saying goes, if you want to make God laugh, tell him your plans. I had spent the past two years really coming to terms with how precious humankind was to God—women included. For a former angry feminist academic from a broken home, this was no easy conclusion, let alone a reality to live by. After I broke up with Ben, I didn't date for a long time. I knew any relationship would probably be on the rebound; Ben and I had cared for each other deeply, and I knew I needed some time. I also wanted very much to get to know better my first love of all loves: God. As trite or as corny as this concept can sound, I meant it earnestly. This King of Hearts was proving a safe bet, I found. I took the verse from Jeremiah 29:13 as a personal compass on this new and exciting journey: "You will seek me and find me when you seek me with all your heart." I began to understand differently why God wanted all of us—not some, or most—but all: "Delight yourself in the LORD, and he will give you the desires of your heart." Amen!

I was intrigued by Christ—smitten, besotted. I spent time in the Word, sought fellowship at my church, and enjoyed the rich company of more and more Christians. I began to have an inkling of what it meant to live one's life "intentionally," a concept that had hitherto been quite foreign to a person from a background like mine—not because I wasn't thoughtful or self-reflective but because like many of us, I was busy surviving, pushing through, or achieving. I enjoyed the odd dinner out or a leisurely stroll through Christ Church Meadow with a male friend here and there, but no one really "rang my bell on Derby Day," as my British friend Hannah liked to put it. This ringless reality, actually, was fine by me. The more I pursued God's company, the more I enjoyed it, and the more I enjoyed it, the more I craved it. At the time, I also felt I had so much catching up to do in terms of living a life of faith—which may have sounded ridiculous to others, especially those who grew up steeped in the faith and have taken things like saying grace before meals for granted. But for someone like me who was new to the Lord's table, everything was wonderful! I loved learning about the Bible stories in more detail and how intricately every detail of the Bible seemed to connect to every other detail. I looked forward to the peace and beauty of evensong at the end of a long day. I marveled at the intimacy of prayer, the taken-for-granted beauty of liturgy, and most of all, how the fallen world, despite darkness and suffering and evil, still somehow tipped more toward the generous than not. Christians, I could clearly see now, had no need of getting high when praise brought such an intense buzz. For buzz it is, when you place your hand on the pulse and power of the living God, as William Wordsworth wrote, and feel:

A motion and a spirit, that impels
All thinking things, all objects of all thought,
And rolls through all things.

In this "honeymoon" of my conversion, there was no room for another lover. Now God's avowed jealousy of the first commandment "You shall have no other gods before me" no longer seemed sullen or unstable, but rather the center on which everything was securely pinned, with a love so powerful—so rolling and impelling and all— that we could hold no other object in the field of our minute perception at the same time.

Of course I thought of TDH from time to time, but I was so busy getting to know God better and pursuing my life in England that TDH seemed a world away. And indeed, with his own life path burgeoning in Washington, DC, he was just that: a world away. We stayed in touch once in a while over email; a witty note here or a spirited theology debate there, but we were far from involved. Every few months, TDH returned to England, at first for some academic detail or another from his studies he still needed to wrap up, and then eventually for trips connected to a British think tank company he worked for in the United States. When these visits occurred, we would gather with friends at a pub or enjoy dinner together at an Indian restaurant. But the visits were never longer than a day or two, and while there was always a "hum" between us, some sort of indescribable electrical current—perhaps a shadow of that motion and spirit that rolls through all things—our conversations, even if alone together and late into the night, never moved past just that: words.

I can't deny how my heart beat faster whenever I happened upon his name in my inbox. Or that my breath caught in my chest whenever I saw his handwriting. And okay, my knees did grow weak when I saw his face across many a crowded pub during one of his visits. Somehow, no one else seemed to have quite the same effect on me. But I didn't pine for him. And I certainly didn't expect to date him, especially in our two very different universes. And I never, ever anticipated marrying him. It's a good thing, however, that God's gravitas is only trumped by his sense of humor. Yes, indeed, life doesn't turn out as planned: sometimes it turns out better.

But there were times, if I'm honest, during those surprise visits, when I was tempted to tempt him. *What would it be like to kiss him?* I would find myself thinking, suspended somewhere above the fray as I stared at his beautiful mouth (his mouth *is* beautiful) while I feigned listening intently to whatever he was saying amidst the din of pints sloshing around me from friends clinking glasses in post-exam-period cheerfulness. *What would it be like to invite him back to my room under the pretense of good conversation,* I would start to think, *ply him with drink, accidently leave one extra button strategically undone, and then . . . ?*

There were times.

But then I would remember verses from 1 Corinthians 6, which seemed an inconvenient backlash of earnestly pursuing God's Word, but also, if I had to admit it again, very timely and, well, *true:* "Do you not know that your bodies are temples of the Holy Spirit, who is in you, whom you have received from God? You are not your own; you were bought at a price. Therefore honor God with your bodies."

And instead of the reminder feeling heavy-handed or holier than thou, it would lead me to think about who my first love truly was, and how I was honoring that love. And, too, how I was honoring another body besides my own possibly involved in the deal. If our bodies are God's, and then are only our spouse's (if the extension of his covenant with each of us allows that), and God rejoices in that relationship—then who am I, of all creation, to put God asunder? Wider culture says my body is my own: I can do whatever I like, any time I like. But Christ culture—or, citizenship in the city of God—says I am the Lord's. I am precious beyond all measure and paid for beyond any price. And so is everyone else. The passport I carry comes with different criteria, and it will take me, even along the way, to a different, always better place.

That being said, sometimes it's hard to keep the destination in view . . .

.ıllıllııı.

"I told him that he should go with you to Guest Night, in my place."

"You did *what*?" I practically spit out my tea in response. Linnea and I were enjoying high tea together at the gorgeous Randolph Hotel for her birthday.

Unperturbed, she continued to pile clotted cream on her warm scone. "I told him that his visit was perfectly timed with Guest Night at your college," she managed to mumble with a mouthful of her sweet handiwork.

"What?" I exclaimed. This had come out of the blue!

She swallowed and then added, "And I told him that you needed a date."

"What?!" I exclaimed again, even louder this time. Then I held my head in my hands. This couldn't be happening. *Ugh. How mortifying!*

"I do *not* need a date, Linnea," I stated as firmly as possible from my state of humiliated agony.

"Yes, you do."

"No, I don't. *You* are my date, remember?"

"No." Linnea looked at me squarely. "I'm a safety substitute."

"What on earth does that mean?" I replied, taken aback.

"You are afraid to date," she stated matter-of-factly.

"No, I'm not," I shot back. "That's ridiculous!"

"Is it?" She arched her brows at me.

"Well . . . " I stammered. "Look, Linnea, I'm really enjoying this time without dating. It's just me and God, you know?"

She laughed kindly. "I know, Caro. But you avoid men. Especially TDH."

"That's ridiculous too," I quipped back. "He's not even around, for goodness' sake!"

"No, it's not ridiculous," Linnea continued to hold her ground. "And yes, he is around—more often than you may realize. Why do you think the guy keeps pinging back to England like a lovesick boomerang?"

My jaw dropped, almost into my own clotted cream.

"You think it's easy or cheap taking jaunts across the pond, Caro? I'm speaking as an American here now myself. It's bank-breaking, soul-crushing, air-miles-sucking work, I tell you. And it's painful for your friends to watch. We love you both, and you both love each other, and we just don't know why you don't get on with it."

I filled the awkward silence by stuffing my face with another warm scone.

Finally, I murmured, "Well, it's not like I'm avoiding him."

Linnea poured herself more tea, then topped up mine. "You, my friend, are hiding behind Jesus' robes."

"That's not fair!" I felt defensive. "Lots of people love Jesus first and foremost. And choose a life in which they love only him."

"This is not whether or not you feel called to be a nun, Caro. That's a whole other gig, and only you know your heart on that one." Linnea reached out and took my hand across the table. "From what you've told me about your faith—and believe it or not, contrary to what you may think and accuse me of, Caro, I *do* listen to you, just maybe not at the time—you Christians are all supposed to love Jesus first regardless, right? But why can't you love Jesus *and* TDH at the same time?"

Suddenly, tears welled in my eyes, taking me by surprise. Holy Spirit tears often do. The cream felt clotted indeed in my throat.

.ılıllıı.

After breaking up with my college sweetheart, I had reconciled myself to the fact that I might never marry, which wasn't really that difficult, if I'm honest, since I actually didn't care to marry. Marriage hadn't turned out that great for my mother, if I was honest yet again, nor had it turned out to be that great for many other women I happened to know. Single mothers working themselves to the bone to put food on the table made up a disproportionate number of the population I knew. Women who had sacrificed their careers, their self-esteem, and their sanity to support men seemed to be the norm in my world, as well as women who were abandoned by those self-same men for younger models of feminine wiles, or traded for market share, or crushed under the wheels of male pride. I knew only too well how the poorest demographic in our privileged North America consisted of older, divorced women. These were women who had lost their earning potential due to having babies, raising babies, and securing the success of those babies with every odd against them of securing their own. In Virginia Woolf's words, "To raise bare walls out of bare earth was the utmost they could do." No, unlike Ruth from the Old Testament story, I had no need of a kinsman redeemer—just the Redeemer would do. I knew many people who hadn't married out of choice, and I certainly respect that decision: it is a personal one for all of us. But I also know that for me, in my own case, the decision was fraught with fears. In avoiding a relationship, I could sidestep intimacy and accountability and responsibility, all the while gleaning what was my share of spiritual inheritance, I was sure. After all, marriage seemed to me to be a high stakes way to be betrayed by a kiss.

Back when studying psychology, I had read an article about how we tend to construct our notion of God based on our experiences with our own fathers. At the time, especially as a skeptic of faith, such a hypothesis stung true: I would have defined my father as intermittent, inconsistent, and incoherent. He could be jovial and indulgent one minute, then sullen or angry the next. At times he could be charming and eloquent, while at other moments, he would rant and rave. What little that I knew of the Judeo-Christian God, I had to admit, seemed pretty similar to me. Take the first commandment, for instance: "You shall have no other gods before me."[6] That seemed pretty moody and self-absorbed too. You could equally have said of my father that he moved in mysterious ways, especially since his breakdown and the bouts with mental instability that followed. Besides, the entire "religious" thing seemed far too risky a bet to place: if I was going to make it, and obviously I was going to have to make it on my own, I certainly didn't have any chips to spare.

I had to admit that the idea of marrying Ben sort of snuck on me; after all, we had been college sweethearts for years. My mother adored him and liked to remind me regularly what a catch he was. A solid, dependable, accomplished guy; Ben was a gentleman too. In fact, when I first became a Christian I was frustrated at how he wouldn't consider giving his life to Jesus too. After all, he was already such a "good guy," why not take the slightest of leaps, or so it seemed to me quite condescendingly, I must add, since I spoke *after* having taken my own leap? It took a bit more maturing in my faith to realize that being "good" has nothing to do with receiving grace, and thank God it doesn't. It also took me a slow boil to learn that, ultimately, there is no rhyme or reason to other people's walks. Some people run, some people amble, and some people crawl toward Jesus—and others in equal approaches go in the other direction. But we all enter the race, whether we are aware of it or not, whether we finish it or not, whether we move away or toward the goal, whether we lose or are victorious. And I was only accountable for me. Of course I would have described myself as committed to Ben, as I know he would have felt the same about me. Part of me was tentative about marrying and even openly cynical (poor Ben!), but part of me was curious, too, and eager to carve my own way, and well, very, very certain of my ability to secure my own success. At the time, however, I had no idea of what marriage entailed for a committed Christian.

Before becoming a Christian, marriage simply seemed to me and many others I knew to be the next step in a committed, serious relationship, sort of like a glorified living together, marked by a beautiful party. Of course both parties were committed: no one marries with the intent of divorce. Marriage in culture at large embodied an agreement dependent upon two parties only, with my happiness (or his, if it happened to really occur to me) as its reference point. After giving my life to Christ, however, I cannot judge another, and indeed we are commanded not to, but in my own heart before God I could not undo what I now knew of what marriage signifies for a follower of Jesus, who reminds us: "I do not give to you as the world gives." Marriage as a covenant before God, one that included God and reflected God—well, that required a whole other type of spiritual maturity and a lifetime of dependence and trust in grace. But once you have tasted the living water, no other sweetness to the soul will do, whether it be for one or for two.

.ılıllıı.

At Linnea's not-so-gentle prodding, then, I invited TDH to the Guest Night at my Oxford college. He was going to be in Oxford for a business meeting that weekend anyway, and it seemed the polite thing to do. All my British friends kept asking about my American date. It's nothing serious, I assured them repeatedly, although I was surprised at how nervous I was!

Guest Night at Oxford University colleges is always a grand affair. But some are more grand than others when the dates happen to conflate with a special occasion, such as a holiday or a college saint's day. A member of a college can bring any nonmember as a guest to dinner on these designated evenings. Dress is formal, dinner is elaborate, and there are often speeches or some sort of entertainment to be enjoyed, followed by drinks in various lounges or common rooms such as the Senior Common Room, which was the comfortable salon where faculty and the master of the college retire. This particular Guest Night marked the start of Advent (the Christmas season in the church), and a grand Guest Night it promised to be!

TDH and I had arranged to meet in the porter's lodge, where I would pick him up and we could make our way together to the dinner hall. I put on my drop-dead, not-so-little-in-front but dramatically-less-in-back LBD, swept up my hair, spent more time than usual on my makeup, and then headed down the long, winding staircase from my dean's quarters to the quad below. When I rounded the corner into the lodge, I couldn't contain my gasp: there was TDH, looking breathtakingly handsome in his full tuxedo. He didn't see me at first as he stood studying a poster on the wall. This gave me the chance to take in all of his form—his tall, dark, glorious all. I felt that familiar flutter in my chest: I say familiar, because, for some reason, I began to realize that it had always been there when he was there. I started to chastise myself for feeling it, but then I thought of Linnea's words, and Jesus' robes, and I decided that instead of ducking behind them I would reach out to touch them, in the hope, just the far off hope, of being healed of a wound the world couldn't see.

TDH turned toward me and our eyes clicked. Until the day I die, I will see him standing in that lodge in the Advent gloaming, hallowed by the Christmas lights strung about and the holly and the ivy in abundance. The halls were indeed decked, and magic flitted through the air like the light snow beginning to fall outside the stained glass window. It felt like standing at the lamppost in Narnia indeed, having passed through the wardrobe and been transported into the beauty of winter. But instead of "always winter, never Christmas," this *was* Christmas, a mere breath away, to be fully enjoyed with its promise of spring, and of the great thaw, just as much inside and outside, to come:

The world is charged with the grandeur of God.

It will flame out, like shining from shook foil;

He came toward me and in a moment scooped me up, literally off the floor, in one of his vintage bear hugs. I felt safe and cherished as he brushed back my loose hair, like he often did, and looked at me intently, asking me questions the entire time about how I had been. He pulled me again into his great chest, and I breathed in his scent deeply, pulling away reluctantly as our friends arrived, beckoning us to join them on the way to dinner.

"Hey, it's Theology Man!" Frazier cried out, coming up and slapping TDH warmly on the back. "Look, he's crossed the pond again. Whatever for?" he smiled at TDH while giving me a wink.

Blushing, I looked away, only to turn quickly back at catching the sweetly distinct scent of violets nearby. *Violets? In the midst of winter?* TDH delighted in my delight as he pinned the corsage of little purple hearts to the front of my dress. Then he spun me around by extending his arm. He gave a low whistle, and pulled me in close again.

"Wow, you look incredible," he breathed in my hair.

"Come on! We don't want to miss the pre-party!" Frazier stepped between us, pulling on my hand while also holding the hand of his date, my very beautiful and incredibly smart friend Maria.

"They are serving wine from the master's reserve tonight as a special treat, but we don't want supplies to run out." He laughed. One could always depend on Frazier to know the quantity and quality of alcohol at a college event.

Reluctantly, I allowed Frazier to pull me into the undertow of guests now swarming toward the dinner hall. *No need to rush,* I thought to myself. I felt intoxicated enough already!

As the dean, I had been invited by the student council to give the speech. Since Guest Night speeches are usually witty, lighthearted talks, and sometimes even roasts—far from the gravitas of formal academic lectures—I decided to do a parody of T. S. Eliot's famous long poem "The Love Song of J. Alfred Prufrock," rewritten with inside jokes about our college life. I also included some fun references to TDH. His appearance as my guest had raised some eyebrows and stares. Many of my friends knew him, but some only knew of him, and with me as the usually professional dean of students who had not hitherto brought a date, he quickly became an object of curiosity. Little did I know how prophetic the theme of a "Love Song" would be. But then again, don't we all underestimate God's good humor with us and his enjoyment in speaking our unique love languages to each of us? Indeed, "God loves each of us as if there was only one of us." Paying attention to the way God speaks to me in my particular love language—that of words, symbols, and literature—has long been a favorite pastime of mine since the gift of conversion and the ensuing holy conversation.

Dinner was delicious, the speech went off "capitally," as the Brits say, and the feting that followed afterward left me giddy from more than just the dance moves. It was late when TDH and I broke away from the hot crowd to stand out in the cold quad upon the hush of newly fallen snow under the night sky generously diamonded with stars. We talked about how nostalgic this event made us feel: our first real "time together" had been back at a Christmas Guest Night at Oriel College over three years ago. I watched how our breath mingled together as we held our heads close to talk. With my bare back exposed to the crisp night air, I shivered. TDH took off his tuxedo jacket and wrapped it protectively around my shoulders. We decided to go back inside.

Together, we climbed the long, winding staircase up to my bed-sitting room at the top of the tower. I took off my corsage so as to preserve it and placed the nosegay of purple violets in a little cup of water on my table. A few friends popped by here and there as the revelry continued through the night, and, ever the artist, Frazier made sure to take our picture. I made good strong North American coffee, and we laughed amidst friends until the last one bid us good-night, and then we were left alone, just the two of us. Again, we talked easily together late and long, as we always had. Soon—oh so much sooner than we ever anticipated!—dawn was creeping up on us:

> And though the last lights off the black West went
> Oh, morning, at the brown brink eastward, springs—

The sound of partying guests down below had dwindled now into a sleepy silence. I got up to collect the empty coffee cups and to take a deep smell of my sweet violets. The Victorians, I knew from my study of nineteenth century literature, were besotted by flowers. Flowers acted as a language of love: a white violet, for instance, meant "innocence," while a purple violet symbolized that the giver's thoughts were occupied with love about the recipient. I smiled to myself as I breathed in their bouquet. Little purple hearts, for courage too. The next thing I knew, TDH had me by my other hand, so that I stood one hand full of violets, one hand pulled close to his chest. I froze. Then, I thawed.

There is my life before Christ and after Christ.

And there is also my life before The Kiss and after The Kiss.

Let it suffice to say that no words could ever do justice to how TDH kissed me that night. Or the effect of that kiss. Or its persistent, consistent, insistent memory.

Such kisses are impossible to describe, so why try? Experience is what leads us from life to death; grace experienced is what leads us from Eden to Heaven. As St. Augustine put it, "Faith is to believe what you do not see; the reward of this faith is to see what you believe." How do I *know* this? Because a kiss is God's ultimate love language: our kiss into being in the Garden of Eden, the kiss of betrayal but ultimate sacrifice in the Garden of Gethsemane, the kiss of restoration in the redeemed Garden of Paradise. Because the faithful will receive a new name upon a white stone of acquittal, a name only known to the recipient and the giver. Because I have watched with new eyes of faith the dawn rise out of darkness.

Because the Holy Ghost over the bent
World broods with warm breast and with ah! bright wings.

Chapter Seven

SWEETNESS TO
THE SOUL

For the body will not only be better than it was
here in its best estate of health, but it will surpass
the bodies of our first parents ere they sinned.

St. Augustine

*E*verything appeared in technicolor that soft, early summer morning as I looked out my garret window like a princess in a tower. I also felt like a princess quite literally since, as dean, my college apartment consisted of the top turreted floor of the back building overlooking the master's glorious gardens girded by a stone wall many centuries old. The sunrise blushed against an electric blue sky, without a cloud in sight. I imagined my love flying to me, again literally, through that sky, from one continent to another, much like the monosyllabic poem "An Aeronaut to His Love" about one flying to his beloved because his feet moved too slow, which TDH had slipped beneath my door only a few short weeks ago.

Those few short weeks ago, I had no idea he was actually in Oxford. The proposal had come as a complete surprise—well, sort of.

Earlier that year, TDH and I had enjoyed our first kiss following our Guest Night date. When I visited his family out in Oregon for Christmas, my mother later told me she knew he was the "one" because I had never missed Christmas at home to be with anyone else, anywhere else, ever. A few months later, TDH visited me in England again for Valentine's Day, using his carefully accumulated air miles to come all the way from Washington, DC, just to have a Romantic dinner with me. We were now dating long distance, formally an "item," and though we had been friends for a long time by now, romantically things were growing serious between us, fast. Serious decisions were popping up everywhere fast too: he had been offered a position with a US/UK think tank, and I had been offered a prestigious research fellowship at another Oxford college, which I was painfully weighing against staying on as dean at my beloved St. Peter's.

With all these variables coming down the pike, I had to admit I got more dolled up than usual for dinner when he arrived last—*it was Valentine's Day, after all*, I reasoned to myself. My hesitations about marrying were slowly disappearing against TDH's steady, Christ-like care of me, and I began to feel swept up in safety, passion, and a deeper love than I ever imagined. I marveled at how marriage could bring together so intimately a man and woman who had not previously known each other but who rested together in Christ. I began to entertain the idea of marriage more and more in this light, and as I did, a thrill traveled through me that I finally began to allow myself to fully feel. Valentine's Day not only seemed a romantic day for a proposal, but it was also the anniversary of my conversion, a fact of which TDH was meaningfully aware.

But when dinner came and went, and TDH gallantly paid the bill, and *still* no small velvet box made an appearance, I sunk back in my chair in dismay. And then I beat myself up for my disappointment. Perhaps I had let my guard down too much? Maybe this was not as serious as I thought? And then, there it was: the serpent hiss in the ear of every woman—the original temptation into thinking one is not good enough. Who was I to have this fabulous man propose to *me*? And, how could I have thought of such a possibility? In response, I grew impatient and irate, because, well, everyone knows that anger feels more powerful than sadness. And so I decided then and there to take care of myself—that this guy would not ruin my chances at a successful future, even if inadvertently, by causing me to drag my heels on the opportunities of life, because of waiting, waiting, waiting... as so many women (my own mother included) had waited on a man (both in time and service) and been wasted on a man (both in body and potential) for ages before me. The old habits are the hardest to kick: the sin of insistent self-sufficiency being perhaps the worst, second only to bitterness.

By spring, then, I had immersed myself in preparing for my doctoral exams and thesis. Where I had been writing TDH letters regularly, I began returning to my academic work instead. Pulling all-nighters to write intense papers became a regular rhythm. On the little sleep I did get, I began dreaming (or was it hallucinating?) of the Romantic authors I was studying. Lord Byron walked in on me (of course) whilst in the shower. John Keats, forlorn as a bell tolling, visited me one night and wondered why I had neglected him so.

In the midst of this state of doctoral pandemonium, I fell asleep very late one night while working. Slumped over my desk in my little turret, I woke to the phone's shrill double British ring. It was Linnea, sounding strangely breathless for, as I noticed on my clock, so early in the morning.

"Caro!" she cried into the phone.

"Linnea!" I yawned back. "It's really early in the morning. Why are you calling me?" I could barely form the words before coffee.

"Wakey! Wakey!" she sang out. "I wanted to catch you before you head to the Bodleian to study."

"That's not for another several hours, Linnea." I was having trouble straightening the kink out of my neck.

"That's irrelevant, Caro. Look, you'll need more time to get ready today."

"No, I won't. I just about finished my edits last night—"

"Not your paper," she cut me off anxiously. "*You.*"

"*Me*? Get ready for what? If you're talking about exams, they are some time off yet—"

Sounding exasperated, she interrupted me again. "Just wear something nice today."

"Why?"

She evaded my question.

"What's wrong with what I've been wearing?" I pressed. Linnea had long been my fashion icon friend: the one with the perfect outfit for any occasion, including a Marquis de Sade masquerade ball (long story). But this seemed pushy, even for her. Then again, I forced myself to look down at the sweats and my Glass Tiger T-shirt from high school I had worn for three days straight. Had I showered? I couldn't remember—finals season at Oxford was always such a blur. Yes, I had showered, I reminded myself between realities—with Lord Byron. How many women could say that? Actually, on second thought, probably a lot.

"You look like . . ." I could hear Linnea taking a deep breath into the receiver.

"Like what, Linnea?"

"Well, Caro, I hate to say it, but . . . you look like a bum."

I tried not to gasp. "I *am* cracking," I partially joked back. "Right down the middle. Do you know I dreamt of Keats again last night? He was upset by my interpretation of Coleridge."

"Caro, you've long been nutters." Linnea's British-isms spoken in her Californian-honeyed voice always made me smile. "First Jesus. Now Keats. Look, I love you, you know that, but I mean it, regardless of your academic prowess, you look like a bum. Please, wear something nice today. Like a skirt."

"You want me to wear a skirt? Are you serious? With three more essay deadlines and sitting all day in the drafty Duke Humphry's room?"

"And shave your legs."

"Now you are the one who's nutters, Linnea."

"For God sakes, Caro, shave your legs, especially with a skirt." Linnea's voice started going up, like it always did when she was frantic. "And wear nice lingerie."

Nice lingerie?

Now she had me suspicious. Something was definitely up. Linnea hailed from New York and LA; she moved in Hollywood circles. Lingerie was code for "prepare for action."

"Linnea . . ."

"Yes?"

"What is it?"

"What's what?"

"What's up?"

"I don't know what you're talking about, Caro."

"You have me nervous . . ." I began.

"Oh, stop being so suspicious," I could practically feel her waving her hand through the phone, brushing off my concerns. She went on quickly, "I just thought you could use a fashion boost. You know, clothes make the man. Or the woman. If you dress well, you'll feel well. You'll perform better. It's proven by research, you know."

Hmm, I had to admit, she might have a point there. I had been feeling like a library slug.

"Well, okay, the change may do me good," I conceded a little.

"And do your makeup."

I was speechless. British girls rarely wear makeup, let alone to the library; they have this natural messy cuteness to them that is utterly disarming and in no need of adornment. Makeup in the United Kingdom is most likely reserved for a night out, and even then it may be weighed against the inconvenience of having your mascara run after a few pints. Linnea's tactics smelled, yet again, distinctly American to me . . .

"Are you still there?" Linnea's voice anxiously broke the silence.

"Yes, yes, I'm still here. Why are you suggesting . . . ?" I ventured.

"And do your hair," she ordered, adding, "Nicely! Put it up. Show a little neck. Okay?"

"Linnea? . . . What the . . . ?"

"Caro, do you love me?" she suddenly said very seriously.

"Yes, of course I do," I spoke calmly. Maybe Linnea was in one of her "fragile" moods; this sometimes happened, especially after one of her mysterious nights out. "You are one of my dearest friends," I assured her, and meant it.

"Then, if not for you, do it for me, Caro. *Please*. Shave your legs for *me*."

"Uh, okay, Lin . . . but . . ."

"I've got to go, sweetie. I'll catch you later for lunch, okay? *Ciao!*"

Before I could say another word, she hung up.

I looked down at my baggy sweats and crisps-stained shirt. So very study-marathon comfy. So very Canadian-undergrad chic. So very, I had to admit, cracked bum.

All right. I decided triumphantly. *I'll do it. Today, for once during finals, I'll be beautiful!*

Upon deciding to run a luxurious bath in the big antique tub down the hall, I went digging around for some scented salts while humming "I Feel Pretty" from *West Side Story.* My mother always hummed appropriate movie tunes in response to real-life situations—I learned and still continue this practice from her to this day.

As I walked into my bedroom, I noticed something sparkled strangely on the floor right inside my apartment door. As I walked closer, I noticed . . . was that . . . *glitter?* How did *that* get there? As I approached closer still, I spied the corner of an envelope peeking out from just under the doorframe. A letter! Someone, at some point, had slipped, sight unseen, a sparkling note under my door. *Wait—I must be hallucinating again!* I told myself. The plague of every overtaxed student—too much caffeine and too little sleep. Had Lord Byron placed it there? Or maybe Keats? I approached with caution. But once standing at the door, I had to admit there at my feet sparkled a real and genuine letter. How had I not noticed its delivery nor its presence until now? How long had it been there, in its cloud of fairy dust? The possibilities were both creepy and exhilarating. Banking on the latter, I picked it up and tore it open. In handwriting heartbreakingly, heart-stoppingly familiar, the note instructed I was to meet the "anonymous" sender of this letter at the statue of St. Bodley outside the library of his namesake, at noon today.

The letter trembled in my hand, showering more glitter to the floor. Suddenly, I *knew.*

Inwardly, I thanked Linnea for waking me so that I had the time to take a hot bath and think. So that I had the prompting to dress nicely, do my hair, perfect my makeup. So that I had, what every woman secretly wishes but would never publicly admit to, the chance to be at least presentable for arguably the most memorable moment of her life. What a friend!

I stared at my bare ring finger while I soaked in the scented bath. I imagined wearing a ring: *his ring.* I felt exhilarated and calm at the same time. And so ready. Heady! Steady. Go!

I feel pretty, oh, so pretty; I feel pretty and witty and bright! And I pity any girl who isn't me tonight.

I dressed (nicely), did my hair (nicely—I couldn't put it up because my hands betrayed me by trembling too much, but I brushed it), applied a little makeup (nicely), and walked otherwise calmly out the door. Waving to the porter as I passed, I stepped lively through the lodge out into the pedestrian flow on the cobblestone sidewalk, winding my way eventually to the quieter side streets and cutting past Worcester College toward the Bodleian Library. As I passed the Radcliffe Camera, I stopped for a moment and sat against the bicycle railing. I took a deep breath. This is it, I told myself. Once I walk through the ancient portico into that quad over there, my life will change. Significantly. I stood up, steadied myself, took another deep breath, and walked through the arch.

The majestic library quad opened up before me, empty and silent, as it tended to be in late morning. The Bodleian sat nestled away, inaccessible and removed from the city core traffic. The usual larger coming and going of scholars tended to fall around opening and closing hours; a small trickle would emerge in about half an hour or so for lunch. Immediately I spotted the stately statue of Sir Bodley gracing the main entrance. I quickly glanced around. No other figure appeared in the courtyard—not one. I looked again, more slowly and carefully, but the quad was empty. I felt my heart drop into the pit of my stomach: maybe I had been wrong? Maybe there had been a misunderstanding on my part? Suddenly, I didn't feel quite so pretty or witty or bright.

Have you met my good friend Maria, the craziest girl on the block? You'll know her the minute you see her, she's the one who is in an advanced state of shock. She thinks she's in love; she thinks she's in Spain. She isn't in love; she's merely insane.

And then, just as I began to list the possibilities in my head for what else the fairy dust letter could have meant, a tall figure emerged from behind the statue. I recognized it immediately, the form was so familiar, so very dear to me. TDH walked toward me, looking straight at me with that sweet lopsided grin of his. My breath stopped along with my heart as rays from the noon sun suddenly climbed over the majestic Bodleian walls, spilling light into the courtyard, illuminating the advancing figure and reflecting off the countless windows, casting brilliant facets everywhere. The moment was truly epic—carved forever in the mantle of my mind! We stood face-to-face, just the two of us, it felt like, in the entire world—only air and light and unspeakable joy all around us!—and then, just as TDH took my hand . . .

. . . the Bodleian Library doors flung open wide and a stream of international tourists poured out of the library into the courtyard. Hundreds of bodies swarmed around us, clicking cameras and calling out to tour guides who responded in various languages.

TDH said something to me that was immediately lost in the babel.

"What?" I replied. "I can't hear you!"

"Are you hungry?" he yelled over the increasing cacophony.

"What?!" I yelled back. I thought I must have misheard him. I had to hold on to him to keep from being dragged apart by the tsunami of human bodies rushing in around us.

"Are you hungry?" he repeated. "Do you want to grab a sandwich?"

I blinked up at him. "You flew all this way to surprise me . . . for a *sandwich*?!"

"Come on!" He slid in tightly next to me and started navigating through the camera-clicking crowd.

Dazed, I allowed myself to be swept along at first. But with each step, I grew more and more mad, and pulled away more and more. *Just what was this? Some sort of sick game? Some sort of "let's see if I can beckon the kitchen wench and she comes at my bidding" stunt?* This was coming particularly close on the heels of the Valentine's Day let down, if you remember. I did.

You always end with a jade's trick. I know you of old. I had to bite my tongue from flinging the Shakespearean insult, the ultimate weapon for a student of English literature. This one was right up with there with *Thou dost infect mine eyes.*

But of course, *he* didn't. It actually felt helplessly good to see him again. While I tried to stay irritated, he bought us a couple of baguettes in a sandwich shop and then pulled me back out onto the street.

"Where are we going *now*?" I asked him in exasperation.

"A picnic," he spoke only two words, looking straight ahead.

A picnic? Is this guy crazy? I wanted to slap him. I was *not* hungry. And I did *not* want a picnic. Confused, I continued to follow along, practically jogging to keep up with his focused fast pace.

"Christ Church Meadow is in the other direction," I reminded him, as he practically dragged me up the High.

"I know." Again, only two more words from him, as he continued looking and striding straight ahead.

Great, I thought.

"I have another spot in mind," he finally turned and said more gently. "Trust me."

Those two words seemed the hardest to take. While vexed, however, I was more curious still. How would he explain this one, I thought? So I nodded. We ducked into New College, which I always found to be such a hilarious British moniker given that it was established in 1379.

"This way," he took my arm again. I wondered why TDH, normally so lively and talkative, was back to two words (at most). He seemed to be acting awfully strange.

Walking quickly past the porter's lodge, he continued to pull me by the hand toward a garden secreting a small but steep hill. Age-worn stone steps picturesquely graced one side, lending the illusion of a classical ruin. The sight took me by surprise, even in a magical place like Oxford, given the whimsical hill's sudden appearance on college grounds and on relatively flat terrain all around at that.

"Welcome to New College Mound!" TDH announced.

"A mound?"

"Yup. And no tourists are allowed here, so we're safe." He winked. "Come! Climb with me to the top." He still had me by the hand. "The view is lovely!"

The view was indeed lovely, and the view, shortly to follow, of TDH on one knee before me, was even lovelier. And what he said, and how he said it, and the way it made me feel and how it made my head spin and my heart sing, well let's just say it was not all due to vertigo . . .

I soon learned that TDH had flown into Heathrow the day before and arrived at Oxford under the cover of night, where he stayed by prior arrangement at the flat of our newly married friends Evelyn and Andrew, who were co-conspirators in his plan. He made sure to call me from their place, making it sound as though he was calling me as usual from his DC residence so as to keep me off the trail. It worked: I never once suspected he was a mere few blocks away! Only three of our close friends knew he was in Oxford: Evelyn, Andrew, and Linnea. He had kept it to a small circle on purpose and they had each been sworn to secrecy. Evelyn and Andrew gave him a place to stay and Linnea was to make sure I was "monitored" and made available. TDH explained how he kept the engagement ring in his pocket for the cross-Atlantic flight, not daring to be separated from it for a moment. He felt its burning presence there the entire trip.

After the ring, and tears, and embrace, and breaths of excitement followed by sighs of satisfaction, TDH brought out from his backpack two glasses and a bottle of champagne. I laughed with delight at the perfect touch, which he had somehow managed to haul along, unbroken, the entire day for this moment. But then I couldn't help teasing him and addressing him by his full name.

"Kent Byron Weber, what would you have done if I had said no?" I asked mischievously.

"Then I would have had a drink to console myself," Kent replied in typical TDH fashion: that is, never missing a beat.

I feel stunning and entrancing, feel like running and dancing for joy. For I'm loved by a pretty wonderful boy!

.·ıllılıı.

At the end of spring term, the master of my college, John, and his wife, Caroline, had gone to great pains to plan the perfect engagement celebration for us. Flowers were everywhere! Tasteful bouquets punctuated the indoor entertaining spaces, while the French doors opened out to a welcoming back garden lush with June blooms. Lattice chairs speckled the lawn amidst small white clothed tables overflowing with strawberries, cream, and champagne. Waiters inconspicuously weaved among guests offering selections from silver trays of fancy hors d'oeuvres. An ice sculpture of two geese flying wing to wing graced the larger center table, with a full tea service including crustless sandwiches, smoked salmon, and exotic fruits situated within an array of cheeses and other delicacies. A string quartet sweetly played Vivaldi on the patio. I was a scholarship girl from a poor background for whom Brie cheese was a treat to be had only at Christmas and who had played classical music on my mother's antique record player. The scene took my breath away.

TDH was scheduled to arrive the morning of the party. I could barely sleep the night before. I woke early and began counting the minutes until the touchdown of his plane, the minutes on the bus from Heathrow to Oxford, the minutes it would take him to walk from the station to the college, the minutes it would take him to sprint up the long, winding staircase to my turret room and take me in his arms. Everyone I passed on the way to the lodge to get my mail congratulated me and expressed their excitement for the party later that afternoon. Some had met him, some had not yet, but all were thrilled for us. Anticipation brillianced the very air around me; everything appeared shiny and bright! He would be flying—*Why? Sweet love, feet move so slow*—from Washington as usual to Heathrow. Poor guy, literally, as he was just about bankrupted by our long-distance romance: every date cost an economy transatlantic fare. He grew up without any Brie at all. If any man deserved to expect sex upon arrival, it was him. But he never expected, only protected.

There are men like that, I would later remind our daughter. *There are.*

Sometimes through faults of our own, however, and sometimes through no faults of our own, we do not, or cannot, show up. His arrival time came and went, but no phone call from Heathrow announced he was on his way. I carefully put up my hair in the comb Linnea gave me, applied the makeup my sister had sent. I stepped back and admired my work in the mirror: my impeccably put-together friend and sister would both be proud of me. I slipped on the Laura Ashley dress selected especially for the occasion by my mother, no easy feat for her either, a single mom on a limited income—just the overseas postage itself guaranteeing the package would make it on time constituted a small fortune. I strapped on the new sandals:

another treat by post from my sister-in-law, as we wear the same shoe size. Even those who couldn't be with me at this first celebration in England were with me in spirit through gifts and cards until we would be among them to be married on the other side of the pond. Finally, all ready, powdered and perfumed, and exhilarated beyond compare, I sat by the phone and waited. Nothing. I made endless cups of tea, never going out of the range of being able to hear the telephone ring. Nothing. I looked at my watch: he should be walking to me by now over cobblestones—I imagined him running!—but perhaps he just forgot our agreement to call, to touch base from the airport once here? That must have been it. I stood up and stretched, having to go to the loo after all that tea.

Finally, the phone rang its double British ring.

"Hi, sweetheart," the familiar voice, both sexy and boyish at the same time, filled my ear.

"Are you calling from the airport?" I blurted out right away. I missed him so much it hurt.

"Yes—" he began.

"Well, good!" I cut him off. "But you'll have to hurry . . . catch the next bus possible . . . I thought you would be here by now!"

"I can't catch the bus," he tried to explain.

"What? Is the service down from Heathrow? Well then, just jump on the train," I suggested, all chipper.

"I'm not at Heathrow," TDH said quietly.

"You just said you were at the airport." I suddenly felt very uneasy.

"I am. Just not that one." He sounded more boyish than sexy by now.

"What do you mean?" I managed to squeak.

"I'm still at Dulles, Caro. There's been a mechanical issue with the plane. We've been delayed and delayed . . ."

"What?" I gasped. "Why didn't you let me know earlier?"

"I didn't want to worry you." I could tell he was staying calm for my sake. "The airline kept delaying things about a half hour at a time. By the time the delay looked more significant, I tried my best to get another flight, but there were none. It was the middle of the night. I tried everything, Caro . . ." His voice trailed off into despondent silence.

"There must be another flight! Another option," I cried frantically.

"No, no other flights. Trust me, I've spoken with everyone at United Airlines all night." I could feel his frustration over the phone.

"But the party! Everyone is waiting to meet you. My whole British family is here!" I lamented.

I heard him sigh heavily across the line. We shared a stunned silence for a few moments. I was grateful he was safe; I was grateful it was nothing more serious. Still, my eyes burned with tears, in spite of myself.

"Look, I'm sorry," I finally croaked. "I know this is hard for you too. You must be exhausted."

"Yeah," he said angrily, though not at me, "I haven't slept a wink. But look, don't panic yet," he added urgently. "There's still time. I have an idea."

"Are you crazy? There is no time. The party is later today!" I exclaimed.

He didn't say anything. For a brief shining moment, I thought this must be a practical joke. I thought it must be the same tactic he took with the proposal—pretending to call me from a distance when he was actually in town.

"Please don't joke about this," I finally managed to say.

"I wish I were," I heard him reply, from, I had to admit, somewhere that sounded far away. I knew from his tone, too, he meant it. This was no repeat on the proposal surprise strategy. My heart fell.

"I have a plan," he managed to say optimistically. "Don't give up hope yet. I will get to you, I will. Okay?"

"Okay," I slowly agreed.

"Go downstairs and have fun with your friends for a bit; say hi to everyone for me," he instructed. "I will call you again in half an hour."

"Okay," I agreed again, glumly. We hung up.

Downstairs, friends and colleagues congratulated me and expressed their excitement at meeting TDH soon. Very generously, John and Caroline had invited everyone in the college to the party. Even the porters and scouts were coming, which made me happier than ever, as I considered them family as well.

I leaned over the shelf and told the porter about TDH's travel delays. "It's not looking likely, Paul."

"Oh that's a shame, luv! You must be on pins and needles."

I nodded, fighting back tears again.

"It will be fine, luv. He says he has a plan. Never underestimate a bloke in love," Paul gave me a wink. "Don't give up hope yet. Don't you worry either. You'll see. Whatever happens it will be fine in the end."

TDH did call a half hour later as promised, but still the update was merely, "I'm working on it."

For the next several hours, I fielded inquiry upon inquiry about updates on TDH's travel status. It was the buzz all around college. I smiled bravely through it all, holding my head high. He would be coming, I told myself over and over. Somehow, some way, he will come.

Frazier, the college wit and insanely talented artist, one of my dear friends and a gentle prodder of "perfect Theology Man," tried humor to relieve the tension.

"See," he said, deadpan. "I knew he didn't actually exist."

Hannah—always my loyal Hannah—jabbed him in the ribs for me.

"I'm sorry this isn't looking good, pet." She turned to me, putting her arm around my waist. "Let's go back to your room and see if there are any messages."

We walked back upstairs together. My heart leapt as I opened my door and spied the blinking red light on my desk phone. I berated myself for having stepped away for so long. I beelined for the phone while Hannah put on more tea, the quintessential British tonic for handling any situation. At this rate, however, I would be peeing nonstop all day.

My finger trembled as I pressed play on the voicemail.

The message simply said: "I'm still trying, my love."

.ılıllıı.

About an hour before the party, the phone rang again. I sprang up to answer it, with Hannah close at my side. Linnea had joined us in my room, as had Frazier, Evelyn, Andrew, and, of all people, Edward, who actually appeared the most pained.

TDH spoke on the other end of the line, sounding utterly exhausted. He wasn't coming.

I listened wordlessly to his diatribe against the airline. And to his desperate attempt from every angle to make a flight in time. He had even gone so far as to try to purchase a flight on a Concord—a $5,000 ticket that would have taken up his entire line of credit on his student Mastercard. No small consideration for a poor pastor's son just striking out in the world during a recession, to say the least. But the Concord wasn't possible, either. It was a Romantic if not very practical gesture. As disappointed as I was at him not joining me for our engagement party, I was secretly relieved that his credit hadn't taken such a hit with our wedding coming up in a few short months, on top of the cost of US immigration fees for me. When TDH finally finished his anguished report on having exhausted every option, he sighed deeply. I could practically see him rubbing his eyes.

"I'm sorry, Caro," his voice cracked. "I feel sheepish and frustrated and upset beyond words. I'm so, *so* sorry."

I swallowed my disappointment.

"It's okay, it's not your fault," I assured him.

"I feel just terrible," he sounded near tears as well.

"So do I . . ." Just when I couldn't say any more, the receiver was suddenly yanked from my hand.

"But we will make the most of it!" Hannah spoke confidently into it. My friends had gathered around her as she held the receiver up for all to hear.

"We will take lots of pictures!" Frazier called out. "I'm an excellent photographer, remember."

"And we'll give you a full report! Including all the gossip!" Linnea added, clapping her hands.

"And we'll make sure your girl has someone on her arm all night," Edward stated tongue in cheek, "You know, to keep the wolves at bay."

Hannah rolled her eyes.

"But seriously," Hannah assured TDH in her most motherly voice, "we will make sure Caro has a fabulous time, and then we will have all we can ready for you to enjoy when you get here next."

After TDH's still mortified but somewhat more comforted farewell, I made my way down to the party with my circle of devoted friends. John and Caroline were terribly sympathetic when I explained to them TDH's necessary absence.

"Oh dear," Caroline consoled me, "these things happen, my dear. But wait, I have an idea! Quickly, bring me every photo you have of him!"

I ran back to my room as fast as humanly possible in heeled sandals and collected what I could. Then, holding my shoes on the way back instead of wearing them, I returned even faster to Caroline. With only an hour left before the party was to start, she hurried out with the few pictures in an envelope.

"What are you up to?" I asked her, intrigued.

"You'll see," she smiled her sweet smile at me.

A short time later, Caroline was back and madly dashing about, plastering copies of the pictures of TDH—alone in some, the two of us together in others—everywhere, including between fine works of art on the walls, by place settings and bathroom soaps, hanging from chandeliers inside, and tree boughs outside. She had even made a life-size portrait of his head and affixed it to a stick.

"Here, carry this with you," she instructed with matter-of-fact cheerfulness. "Whenever someone wants a picture, just hold this up next to your face."

"That's a little freakish," Frazier, our event photographer, whispered to me. "But very sweet."

As the guests poured in, Caroline's enthusiasm became contagious: the epitome of a dignified good time, she banished any awkwardness or disappointment. We all started passing around TDH in good fun. Caroline started a game in which we all shared stories about him and even imagined what he would say to such a comment or to such a question. Everyone had a lovely time, and TDH was deeply touched by being included in the memorialization as well. In all my photos of the evening, TDH was "there."

A week later, TDH arrived on a flight that the airline provided free of charge, given that he missed his own engagement party due to their delay tactics. After everything they had already done, John and Caroline insisted on taking us for a beautiful dinner, just the four of us, to celebrate. As we thanked them at the end of their meal for their generosity (yet again), I complimented John in particular on his wife's ingenuity.

"She really saved the day!" I smiled as Caroline patted my hand. An accomplished academic in her own right, she had raised two wonderful children with the erudite yet affable master. I knew I would remain forever inspired by their example of intelligence *and* fun.

"Sometimes a man may seem to be absent," John said to me as he smiled at Caroline. "But when it comes to his beloved, he is there, my dear girl. No matter the distance or obstacle or seeming appearances of things, in our hearts we blokes are *there*." Then with his usual wit, he offered to refill my glass with his go-to phrase, "More madeira, my dear-ah?" before calling for a toast congratulating the happy and reunited couple.

"We are sorry to see you go, Carolyn." John put his hand on mine warmly. "But alas, it is for a good cause."

I smiled back at him and squeezed his hand, tearing a little as he was like a father to me. His eyes grew misty, too, and he turned quickly then to TDH, saying, "And if you have even a smidgen of the joy I have had with my own Caroline, you will be a blessed man indeed."

"Indeed, sir," TDH said warmly back.

"Oh, here!" Caroline placed an object on the table in front of us, for she was growing teary now too, and in typical British fashion, the upper lip must not quiver and so protocol called for the interruption. It was one of TDH's pictures from the engagement party, still attached to a straw.

"A memento," she announced. "It never hurts for a wife to keep her husband's head on a stick."

.ılıllıı.

That October had been unseasonably warm, with thunder rolling almost constantly in the distance and the air as heavy as water. *It's like rain on your wedding day,* I could practically hear Alanis Morissette singing in my ear, just like the last time I arrived in the capital of the United States. TDH and I were to be married in Washington, DC, on

Sunday evening of the long holiday weekend convenient to both countries from which we, and our visiting families, hailed: Columbus Day in the United States and Thanksgiving in Canada. TDH's home church, Capitol Hill Baptist, graciously hosted the wedding, everyone welcoming me there as though I had been attending my entire life. Ladies took me out to find a wedding dress, got me settled in my new apartment, and helped me find an affordable cake and catering. It had been very difficult to find a venue for the reception, however, especially on such a tight budget and in a buzzing social city such as DC. Our decision to go with a Sunday night gave us the middle of a long weekend to enjoy our guests and allow them to travel more leisurely and made available a beautiful ballroom in Maryland at a very reasonable price, since Sunday evenings were rarely booked. We even received leftover supplies from the wedding the Saturday before at no cost. As a young couple starting out with nothing to our names (I couldn't even bring my tea kettle from England, as it worked on a different voltage), we were in heaven with gratitude and excitement at the provision!

For all of September and October in that sweltering DC heat, TDH would take the subway and then walk several blocks from the station to my apartment (the one we had leased together where he would join me after the wedding) carrying a bouquet of flowers (or "mad handfuls," as he would say, paraphrasing Cyrano de Bergerac). I was beginning to panic that there seemed no end in sight of the unseasonable heatwave: my wedding dress, with long lacy sleeves and a full skirt, had been chosen in light of anticipated later fall temperatures. My future mother-in-law had gifted me with a gorgeous, woolen, long dress in the color of my bridesmaids' dresses for the rehearsal dinner, but I feared now I would not be able to wear it. For weeks leading up to the wedding, TDH brought me roses almost every day.

I kept every single one, carefully hanging them up to dry in my little apartment hall closet since they wilted quickly in the heat. Without letting on to TDH, I made wreaths out of them as centerpieces for our reception tables. When I finally revealed my handiwork to him a few days before the wedding, he couldn't believe his eyes.

"You made those out of the flowers I brought you?" He hugged me close, clearly touched by the gesture.

"Yes," I said excitedly. "Every single one." I had to admit, the dried roses in the bramble wreaths suited the autumn season and gave a romantic Victorian feel to the occasion.

"They are lovely," he breathed into my hair. "And so are you."

As we embraced, I distinctly remembered thinking: *I don't care where we marry, or how we marry. I don't care if the earth caves in or the venues burn down. I don't care if a drought melts us or a freak snowstorm hits and closes down the city. I don't care if everything that can go wrong does. I just want to marry him.*

The heatwave continued right up to the day of our rehearsal. Family arriving from out West and Canada were met with an un- expected wall of humidity upon exiting Dulles Airport. Friends set up fans in the church as the bridal party sweated through our practice service. Sadly, I couldn't wear the woolen dress from my future mother-in-law. My sister and I ended up dashing out madly at the last minute in search of sleeveless dinner dresses as a thunderstorm threatened again. My father showed up, but due to his increasing poor health, I didn't think he would be able to walk me down the aisle. I held my breath, unsure what to expect from him emotionally as well, but he remained unusually docile though often disoriented. It took many practice steps with him at the church rehearsal, and I knew the actual aisle moment would be shaky at best. There was a confusion with my wedding cake order from the Chinese bakery.

And TDH's old Jetta died in the heat on our way to pick up the wine. But I didn't care: for a bride-to-be, I strangely lacked the jitters. *I just wanted to marry him.*

Early on the morning of my wedding day, I awoke in my little apartment with my loyal bridesmaids who had traveled so far to be with me, all still asleep. When I opened the front door, in swept a cool breeze. The heatwave had broken! Clear skies stretched above me. I would be able to wear my lacy long sleeves in the perfect temperature. Later that evening, after our vows, we would walk down the street from the church to the lit-up Capitol for our wedding photos in absolutely ideal conditions. We had weathered the heat, the storm, the pressure of time, and come through to blue sky! Foreshadowing indeed.

When I picked up my mail upon returning from our honeymoon, included was a package from two of my students from Oxford, Marney Parker and Ben Arnoldy. I had taught them as visiting American students in a British undergraduate literature tutorial. These delightful students had born witness to my burgeoning romance with TDH; they held a special affinity for him as fellow Americans. Inside was a poem they wrote, replete with witty references to all the works we had studied together. They had it framed, a treasured gift I still have on my wall today:

An Ode to Carolyn and Kent

October 12, 1997

Let us go then, you and I
While the night is stretched out against the sky
For a walk down memory lane.
We start in Oxford, at Oriel College
Where our heroine, Carolyn,
Left the Room of Her Own, to meet a Man of Mode.

(Is he a bird? Is he a plane? No, he's Kent.)
She Stooped to Conquer
And became a Woman in Love.
Then Kent left to justify the ways of government to man
And went Sailing to Byzantium.
Sadly, he slew an albatross, Nature took revenge,
And he ended up in Washington, DC.
Carolyn, with her Paradise Lost, returned to a Room
    of Her Own,
This time in Besse, at St. Peter's College.
There she met a few American Pilgrims
Who under her guidance, made much Progress.
Kent came to visit several times;
The one Good Friday, 1997: Riding Eastward,
He stopped in Oxford, whisked her up a hill,
Fell to his knee, and asked,
"Will you marry me?"
(An ecstasy of fumbling!)
"Do you dare to eat a peach?"
And—Paradise Regained!—she said yes.
A celebration was to be held.
We all waited for Godot to show. He didn't,
And neither did Kent. (Blame the airlines)
But the lovers were soon reunited.
And one autumn day they gathered everyone together,
Some from as far as the Castle of Toronto,
To share with them their long awaited wedding day.
And it was a Capitol event indeed!
Old father, old artificer, stand these lovers now and ever in
    good stead.

Chapter Eight

SEA OF LOVE

Love, and do what you will. If you keep silence,
do it out of love. If you cry out, do it out of love.
If you refrain from punishing, do it out of love.

St. Augustine

Old father, old artificer: has it really been over twenty years since you stood us in good stead?

We were moving house—again.

My father died a few months back, and with his birthday now looming, I felt the heavy sorrow of the year of "firsts."

I kicked at the pile of boxes that seemed to always move with us but remain unopened. Probably the only worse packrat in the world after me is my husband. Usually I just blindly moved the same boxes every time, but for some reason on this afternoon, standing there in the sweltering heat of the open garage, I decided to open one and take a look inside. Perhaps it came from a subconscious desire to procrastinate, or perhaps it was just a reason to sit after a long, dusty, hot summer's day spent lifting and shifting, packing and taping. The first box opened easily; Christmas crafts cherished from the children's early years winked up at me amidst tinsel and tree ribbon. How little hands seemed to make those keepsakes only yesterday!

And then suddenly, also as if it was only yesterday, small children are knocking on my bedroom door. In my mind, it's the New Year's Eve the year before my father's fatal fall, just a week after our very special Christmas together. The kids keep knocking and so their daddy and I let them in. Our four young children pile onto our king size bed—our marriage bed, unmade and messy, but ours alone and safe.

"Tell us again how we were born, Mommy!" cried out one of the twins. They love hearing their birth story: how their deliveries straddled midnight, resulting in two different birthdays. They were in their matching Dr. Seuss Thing One and Thing Two pj's a friend had made them.

"No, Mommy, go back before that!" our oldest, our only daughter, demanded. "Back before even me!"

"That's a long time ago," the littlest one remarked, eyes wide.

"Yes, Mommy, to when you and Daddy married. Before you married! How did Daddy propose?" she insisted.

"Was it Romantic?" the other twin asked.

"Yes, very Romantic." I sighed.

"I know it was on a hill. And that daddy had a backpack with champagne," our daughter stated authoritatively.

"What's *sham-pain*?" the littlest one peered up at me, snuggling closer. Everyone, in fact, vied to snuggle closer. The bed of post-Christmas children excited about New Year's Eve now resembled a sack of squirming puppies.

"*Champagne* is a drink with lots of little bubbles in it," I said as I kissed his forehead.

"Like ginger ale, but for adults," his sister explained, omnisciently.

"Have you ever taken it off? Your special ring, Mommy?" Thing Two asked.

"Nope," I conceded.

"Not even to clean it?"

"Not even to clean it."

"Ew, gross," he proclaimed. I raised my eyebrows, given that this was the messiest of all my kids passing judgment.

"I brush it at times on my finger to clean it. I don't think I could take it off now even if I tried. But I don't want to. It's part of me."

We all enjoyed a satisfied silence.

"Diamonds are mashed dirt, you know," our daughter suddenly stated matter-of-factly. "*Compressed.*"

"Really?" I replied, a split second before realizing how she meant this.

"Really. We learned it in science class. Carbon is found in soil and plants," she explained patiently.

We all took this in as well.

"So I guess it doesn't matter if you clean it or not then, Mommy." Thing One finally piped up.

"Why would you wear confessed dirt on your finger?" the littlest one asked.

"*Compressed,*" Big Sister corrected Littlest Brother.

Unfazed, he repeated his main point: "Dirt."

"Why, Mommy? *Why?*" he pleaded. My kids are the Kings of Why. Especially when they are trying to evade bedtime.

"Honey, I don't know why people wear diamonds in engagement rings," I had to admit. "Perhaps because it's a type of promise, like the ring itself, of what we can become. When I look at my diamond, I am reminded of what we were created to be."

"Huh?" replied the little brothers in unison.

Big sister flashed them a knowing look: "It's kinda like dirt realizing it had finally become a diamond."

Her brothers smiled back at her.

"Yeah, honey," I smiled too. "Pretty much like that."

.ılıltlıın.

As we snuggled on the bed together, I told my children about the fairy dust and the letter slipped under my door, and about the Bodleian statue, the outpouring of tourists, Plan B, and *sham-pain*. My son examined my ring again when we got to that part in the story, and how Dad said the ring had burned a hole in his pocket the entire red-eye flight from DC to Heathrow.

"That must have hurt," Thing One observed.

"Love hurts, sometimes," Thing Two replied with all sincerity. He tended to repeat things from the car radio.

The littlest one soon slept soundly in the crook of my arm but the older ones still had some fight left in their eyelids. So I settled into the story of Dallas and Edie, the first folks we met as an officially married couple other than those on our wedding guest list.

"Was his name actually *Dallas*?" Our daughter looked at me suspiciously.

"Yes, it was," I assured her. "And he resembled Dallas too."

"How can someone resemble Dallas?" she asked, still unsure.

"Well, everything about him was bigger than life: big car, big laugh, big hug, big hat. He had this really warm way about him, with a kind Southern accent, and a sweet gentility."

"And Edie?"

"She was as cute as anything. And very Texan too: big hair, big jewelry, big smile, big heart. She made us our first martinis."

"What's a *mar-teenie*?" Thing Two asked sleepily.

"It's another Big Person drink," his sister answered for me. "*Texan*," she added, knowingly.

"It sounds small," Thing One commented.

"It is. It's a small drink for big people," I explained. First, *sham-pain*, now a *mar-teenie*; this was not the kind of conversation I anticipated with my young children on New Year's Eve. I decided to change the topic quickly.

"So, Dallas and Edie were neighbors to Daddy's friend, who was very kindly letting us stay in his Florida condo for our honeymoon," I began. "And generous it was, as Daddy and I barely had a dime to rub between us." I smiled fondly at the memory. But then I realized things weren't much different now, with our four children including a set of twins and a surprise baby later, and moving yet again to another country.

"Florida sounds nice." Our daughter sighed in the midst of our Canadian January.

"It is. It was. We were very blessed to have this beautiful place right on the beach. Since Daddy's friend was gone, he had left instructions for us to get the key from Dallas and Edie. This nice, old couple also offered us the use of their car—a big ol' Cadillac, with a set of steer horns on the hood."

"Wow . . ." the kids crooned together.

"Yes-sir-ee. Daddy was hoping to get the key from them kinda quickly, however, and get into our apartment to be alone."

"Why?" a small voice asked.

"Because we were . . . tired, sweetheart," I explained.

"Did you need a nap?" It asked again.

"Yes, that's what we wanted. To climb into bed," I explained coyly. "We had just arrived from the airport, and not even married a day. But in order to get the key—"

"I always need a nap after we travel all day to see Grandma and Papa," Thing Two concurred.

"We had to visit with Dallas and Edie. You see, they—" I tried to continue.

"Did you and Daddy have one bed then too?" Thing One interrupted.

"Yes. We did. But Dallas and Edie . . ." I tried yet again to pick up the thread, "they wanted to have a proper visit with us—"

"I'm sorry you still don't have enough money for two beds, Mommy." Thing One sighed.

"That's okay, hon." I had to smile. "I don't mind sharing with Dad."

"Except when he snores."

"Yes, except when he snores."

"What did Dallas and Edie do when you came over?" One could always count on our daughter to keep track of the thread.

"Well, to your father's dismay," I smiled, "they put out cheese and crackers—"

"That was nice."

"Yes, very nice."

I smiled at the memory of my very newlywed husband's pained look when Dallas insisted we get comfortable, and Edie showed up first with the tray and then with the pitcher.

"And then they insisted we have a drink with them too," I continued.

"Oh, I know, those teeny-tiny martins."

"Martinis," his sister corrected him.

"Why not *sham-pain*?" He looked at her.

"Martinis are sophisticated," I answered. "A bit strong for my taste, but it was kind of them to offer. We didn't want to be rude, so even though the drinks were kinda yucky, we tried to drink them."

"Did you make the same face you make when you drink Auntie Wendy's coffee?" Thing One asked solemnly.

"Probably, when I come to think of it. Daddy tried really hard to finish his drink, but then he had to make an excuse to go to the bathroom, and he poured his out there." We all giggled at the sneakiness of it.

"What about you?" Thing One persisted.

"I managed to finish mine," I admitted. "But then again, I like olives; Daddy hates them."

"Are there olives in *mar-teenies*?" He looked at me with genuine concern.

"Yes, if they're dry," I said.

"Aren't drinks wet?" he grew more alarmed.

"Ew, gross. I hate olives too!" his twin chimed in.

Realizing that this story wasn't inducing sleep as quickly as I originally thought it might, I changed tactics again.

"Okay, enough questions, and no more chatter now, kiddoes. Just listen and rest your eyes," I spoke more quietly, tucking the three remaining sleep-fighting children back into the blankets around me.

"Now . . . where were we?" I started again.

Our daughter wriggled importantly: "You and Daddy really want the key to the fun condo so you can nap together and then drive the fun car with the antlers but you have to drink dry drinks—I still don't get how something wet can be dry but *oh-kay*?—and these drinks taste like Auntie Wendy's coffee and then Dallas and Edie bring out crackers and cut the cheese—"

"*Coupe de fromage*!" Both boys suddenly interrupted their irritated sister with a phrase learned from French class, chanting it over and over again with typical little boy humor at any euphemism for "fart."

"Get it, Mommy? Dallas and Edie cut the cheese!" They rolled around in hysterics.

"Okay, okay, kids, clearly you are not getting sleepier," I repri-manded them. "I don't want you waking your little brother. Please, boys, settle down! Let's call it a night."

"Oh please, Mom! Not yet, it's New Year's Eve!" They all cried out again in unison. "We'll be quiet. We promise. Continue the story! Pleeease!"

Their eyes were so puppy-dog plaintive, and their voices so kitten-mewingly urgent, that I finally relented. Settling back all to-gether in the big bed, their littlest brother snoring soundly amidst all the chaos (just like his father), I continued to share details from the honeymoon: the warning signs posted about alligators in the parking lot; the dangerous jellyfish manifestation our second day there, which rendered the beach off limits for the rest of our stay; eating grouper every night in the elegant restaurant downstairs, which was painfully expensive for our budget but oh so delicious! And how the little flavored pats of butter that came with the bread were arranged in various shapes. I told them how the monarch but-terflies from our region here in Canada were completing their mi-gratory circle right outside our condo window overlooking the Gulf of Mexico. I sighed at the memory of waking up to roses spilling over the bedside table from Daddy, with a small card in-scribed with only:

!

And how Daddy's friend had left a beautifully wrapped gift in the kitchen for us upon our arrival, along with a fridge full of exquisite gourmet treats, a bottle of wine, freshly ground coffee, and cream. The gift proved to be a delicate crystal decanter etched with butter-flies, in which I put the fragrant red roses. On those rose-colored mornings, I literally awoke to butterflies fluttering in my balcony view: *I through blue sky fly to you . . .*

Imparadised thus in each other's arms, we paid no heed to the stinging beach below.

.ılıIlıı.

The second box in the garage proved more difficult to open. Taped heavily, its seal defied my prying fingers and so I picked up the utility knife on the garage shelf next to me. I didn't expect what was lying right inside the box as I cut it open—I realized almost simultaneously with the slice just how precariously close I had come to inadvertently slashing the delicate contents exposed right at the top.

Packed inside was my collection of nineteenth-century books from my now late dad. The box remained intact from the previous move because we hadn't been here long enough to unpack it. As I picked up the first volume and began leafing through it, a picture fell out. I caught my breath as I recognized the scene: my parents gathering near TDH and me right after the wedding service. In the fresh grief of seeing my father's image again, I let the picture fall to the ground, unable to look at it just yet. Several other loose photos continued to flutter out of the pages as I turned them. I realized that they were all of our wedding weekend: one of my sister arriving, with us hugging at the Dulles airport. Another with my big brother sweeping TDH up in a warm hug. Memories of our wedding ringed around my feet.

I bent down, digging further into the box only to discover a stack of letters from TDH between the volumes. I thought I had most of them safely put away in my jewelry box, but here was another stash secured between some remaining copies of our wedding invitations. Now I remembered that I had put them here for safekeeping in the rush of some previous move. They were gathered together in a larger envelope with a music tape. I couldn't believe it! I had to smile at the real music tape from the eighties, an antique in its own right decades later, along with these old books. I turned it over and gasped at the title: *The Honeydrippers*. Their hit cover of the 1950s classic "Sea of Love" was our wedding song—our first dance as a married couple. I closed my eyes and hummed the lyrics, which came to me instantly, despite the many years since I last heard them. "Come with me, my love. To the sea—the sea of love." Then I opened the first letter:

Dearest Caroline,

Our two hours on the phone tonight was truly lovely . . . You are just so very gracious to me. Please believe me that it never goes unnoticed. After we spoke last night I went in and read your other three letters. Argh! I am absolutely screaming at how lovely you are. Many, many responses could be in order . . . I especially loved the postcard of the puddle-jump that begins, "Almost a week now since we made the leap!" Never a dull expression from Drake the Witster. ☺

Er . . . just for fun, I'm enclosing the short-list (keyword— "short") of the extent of my scant worldly possessions. It won't fill a house, but after a dining room table and chairs and a bed, we should have most of what we need. One part of me is chagrined that you have to marry-in so "low" to get next to me, but then my other side is relieved to know that you can't therefore be marrying me for my money. ☺

I'm racing off to the post office to put your tix in the mail. If I'm lucky, I'll have to jump a puddle and remind myself of the day I made the leap and you came with me. ☺ Life is going to be such a Splash!

All my love,
KBW

Stooping, I retrieved the picture with my parents in it again, determined to look at my father's image now despite the sting of grief. We are not yet posed as a group; the wedding photographer must have still been giving directions because I am looking the other way while my sister fiddles with my dress. My mom's arm encircles my waist but her eyes look faraway and sad, even a little terrified—at the time, I was hurt by what seemed to be her distance, although now I understand so much better, given her own life experience and dreams for her daughter. But it was my father's image, large and bulkily classy in a tuxedo, that held my attention. He is standing awkwardly to the side of the group, waiting to be welcomed in. We are all unaware of the camera, and of him. This day, however, I studied my father's face, who is studying Kent's (or TDH's) face. With an intake of breath, I realized for the first time just how my father is looking at my new husband: with an intensity that is hard to describe, and a sort of, well, *awe*. In my father's slightly turned profile, I detected trepidation, intimidation, protection, and a fierce love for the young man he is holding in his gaze—and perhaps there was a reminder of the young man he once was himself as he stood with equal promise and pride, his eyes bright, his face brimming with the same smile, his bride's arm, too, wrapped safely in his on the steps of the church in his own wedding portrait. My parents' broken dreams lay as scattered now about me as the fragments from this Caesareaned box.

What happens when the sea of love seems more like a puddle of mud? Or a "Slough of Despond," as John Bunyan put centuries ago yet still so relevantly in *The Pilgrim's Progress*? The Romantic poet William Wordsworth wrote:

There was a time when meadow, grove, and stream,
The earth, and every common sight,

To me did seem
Apparelled in celestial light,
The glory and the freshness of a dream.
It is not now as it hath been of yore;—
Turn wheresoe'er I may,
By night or day.
The things which I have seen I now can see no more!

The "Sea of Love" lyrics are replaced by my father's final words, playing again in my head: *Sweetheart, life doesn't turn out as planned.*

.ıllıllıı.

When I stood before the altar with TDH, I promised both him and God that I would honor my husband with my mind, heart, and body, which translates into loving someone unconditionally and completely. At times I find this very difficult to do, and at other times impossible, as I am sure my husband does with me as well—but God holds us in his hands. He is the covenant maker and the covenant caretaker. I can hand over my impossibilities to his possibilities, for nothing is impossible for God. I can rest beneath his wings or between his shoulders. He is my support and my shield. For a girl whose father was not around often and, when he was, he feared comforting her or didn't know how, I now know I share Benjamin's blessing:

Let the beloved of the LORD rest secure in him,
for he shields him all day long,
and the one the LORD loves rests between his shoulders.

In Hebrew, *Benjamin* means "son of the right hand." Benjamin was the baby of the family, the littlest and most vulnerable, and yet the progenitor of the Israelite tribe of Benjamin. When my father lay dying and could no longer communicate, I held his right hand, purposely, for weeks in the ICU. I am a daughter of the right side too. In Christ's blood shed for me, I am buoyed by the salt of the truth and washed clean by the water of forgiveness. The Big Sea of Love holds me in its ebb and flow. Here, I am not forgotten; here, I cannot drown.

The sins of the father do play out for generations: everyone brings both the good and the bad, the helpful and the not-so-helpful, into the present from their past. Patterns in childhood play out in adulthood, and most surface in our places of greatest intimacy and so of greatest vulnerability. Yet no matter how we plan, we cannot control anything beyond our own thoughts or reactions, nor can we extend our lives by one moment. Perhaps the physical attraction we feel in our youth is there to draw us toward the one we will build a life with, whom we will come to know more intimately than any other human being in the world? Perhaps sex in marriage girds us for the forgiveness to come: the granting in advance, the "fore" of the giving:

> When you are old and grey and full of sleep,
> And nodding by the fire, take down this book,
> And slowly read, and dream of the soft look
> Your eyes had once, and of their shadows deep;

Growing old together, intimacy between bodies wrinkled and worn, with stretch marks and grey hair (or no hair) and warts and all, owning the privilege of knowing another as you know yourself, and so resting fully and easily in the dearest company in the world—this, all this, is the crowning glory of giving and giving and giving in advance.

"Being in love is a good thing, but it is not the best thing," C. S. Lewis stated. "There are many things below it, but there are also things above it." It is a noble feeling, but still a feeling, and no feeling lasts. This intense initial excitement is not sustainable, nor would we really want it to be. But, as Lewis teaches, ceasing to be "in love" need not mean ceasing to love. Of her first year as a widow after forty years of marriage, Joan Didion wrote: "This will not be a story in which the death of the husband or wife becomes what amounts to the credit sequence for a new life, a catalyst for the discovery that . . . 'you can love more than one person.' Of course you can, but marriage is something different. Marriage is memory, marriage is time."

For our wedding, my mom-in-law had the famous passage about love from 1 Corinthians 13 printed on bookmarks that were distributed at the place settings. The words have been so overused as to seem cliché. Even though I was touched by the gesture, I remember thinking they were even "cheesy" at the time. But this is the cultural problem with Scripture; it gets tossed around so much it appears threadbare, even ridiculous. However, just because words are worn do not mean that they still don't fit. Not really letting Scripture sink in, no matter how superficially overused, is a bit like throwing the baby out with the bathwater, or the marriage out with the wedding.

> Love is patient, love is kind. It does not envy, it does not boast, it is not proud. It does not dishonor others, it is not self-seeking, it is not easily angered, it keeps no record of wrongs. Love does not delight in evil but rejoices with the truth. It always protects, always trusts, always hopes, always perseveres.
>
> Love never fails.

What gall had we young folk to throw such words around, with such bloated popularity? What nerve had we to use them as a trinket at a wedding? Maybe my mom-in-law, thirty years down her own marriage line, however, knew something we didn't. Back then, as hour-long newlyweds, we had *no* idea. A quarter century later, we still had no real idea. Sitting there with my own shortcomings, I had to admit that I had nothing even *close* to an idea. *Father, forgive them, for they know not what they do.*

Father, forgive *me.* For it was only this past year that I plucked the token wedding bookmark from its sauce-spattered place on the fridge and inserted it in my Bible. I held the same bookmark in my hand now, my Bible open on my lap, in the quiet, still house—married but alone. I intended to read my devotional and Bible, as usual, in tandem. But instead I kept fidgeting with the bookmark in my hand. I studied the wedding-worn words with new eyes. Then I glanced at my devotional.

"Obedience is not so much a keeping to the rules as acts of selfless love," discerned Lucinda Vardey. "Obedience is an honouring: it opens the doors to opportunities to serve God without personal desires."

Henry Drummond, over a century ago, recognized the same struggle:

> In Britain the Englishman is devoted, and rightly, to his rights. But there come times when a man may exercise even the higher right of giving up his rights. Yet [the apostle] Paul does not summon us to give up our rights. Love strikes much deeper. It would have us not seek them at all, ignore them, eliminate the personal element altogether from our calculations. It is not hard to give up our rights. They are often external. The difficult thing is to give up *ourselves.*

Personal desires are not at the heart of intimacy. Rather, selfless acts of love are. Realizing that we are part of something bigger than ourselves reorients us toward what really matters. Otherwise, empty sex, like empty everything else, only leads us to the refrain of Ecclesiastes: "Meaningless! Meaningless! . . . Everything is meaningless." In this light, G. K. Chesterton spoke to the power of two:

Through all this ordeal his root horror had been isolation, and there are no words to express the abyss between isolation and having one ally. It may be conceded to the mathematicians that four is twice two. But two is not twice one; two is two thousand times one. That is why, in spite of a hundred disadvantages, the world will always return to monogamy.

Covenantal sex remembers us. When I am impatient, when I have failed to be kind, when I have grown weary of persevering, when I have lost hope, I can always remember. Jesus offers *his body* to us for just such a remembering: "This is my body given for you; do this in remembrance of me."

When we enter another body, we enter another life. We enter another's joys and sorrows, needs and wants. We fill each other's gaps, to get closer to that other person than our own skin. If my mind will not recall, or my heart cannot, my body will. The old intimacy binds us together. As a psychologist friend of mine explains with trauma as well as with pleasure: the body remembers, the body keeps score.

What should I tell my kids, not just about sex, but also about the wanting to be known inherent in the desire for sex, the being known in the act, the *real* intimacy? That sex is a re-membering? I remember my spouse when I first met him: what attracted me to him, not just physically but as a wonderful human being. I am called to love my spouse and try, every day, to see him as God sees him. As someone who knows him intimately, I imagine him as a child, as a teenager, as a young man embarking on a brave new world . . . the physical act of entering into intimacy encourages the imaginative compassion of entering into another's life. When I lose sight of this compassion, the memory of sex rekindles this connection. Within the protected trust of marriage comes the sacred privacy of sacrament: "The man and his wife were both naked, but they felt no shame."

We all long to be known. And if we are made in God's image, then wouldn't it be safe to assume that God longs to be known too? True knowing takes patience, takes time:

What will become of you and me
(This is the school in which we learn ...)
Besides the photo and the memory?
(... that time is the fire in which we burn.)

Years after accepting it, I spin that same ring on my finger. I know from my days of working in a jewelry store that diamonds are indeed formed from long-term exposure to very high pressure and very high temperatures—in other words, they emerge from the crucible of time.

．．ıllıllıı．

I think back to how each child had finally fallen fast asleep around me on our bed, that eve to a new year now being lived.

"So, sweet ones," I concluded quietly, "to make a long story short—or, well, too late for that I guess—that is how you came to be."

I studied their sleeping forms. Is there anything lovelier than a sleeping child? I think not, especially to an exhausted but adoring mother. I wish I could speak into their dreams. That I could assure them of their birthright to an abundant life.

I kissed the children's heads as their dad came and carried them one at a time off to their own beds. Then I padded back into the living room in my fuzzy slippers (a gift from the kids) and my Christmas jammies (a gift from my husband) to pour two glasses of champagne for us and a bowl of chips. With four young children now tucked in their beds, 'twas a night of high romance. On the television with the sound muted, crowds cheered the countdown to the new year as the ball began to drop in Times Square.

Their father returned and selected a favorite playlist, quietly putting on the music of U2 so as not to wake the kids. Soon Bono sang sweet and low. "I've conquered my past, the future is here at last. I stand at the entrance to a new world I can see." When there are more thorns than roses, more jellyfish than butterflies, more real pain than *sham-pain* . . . when rod and staff seem not enough, "when they no longer comfort me; love, rescue me." Marriage is the mini-me of God's covenant with each of us, regardless of our earthly relationship status. Marriage, washing over me, as it was intended to be, is a sea, a sea of love.

Chapter Nine

THROUGH THE WOODS DARKLY

For [the apostle] Peter was in a healthier condition when he wept and was dissatisfied with himself, than when he boldly presumed and satisfied himself.

ST. AUGUSTINE

With a book deadline looming and a stack of grading during the height of midterm exam season, I took a friend up on her kind offer to let me use her cottage at a nearby lake for a brief retreat. For October, the leaves beat unseasonably green against an azure sky. The pavement ahead shimmered with heat, creating a mirage that disappeared as I lowered my speed and pulled into the little beach community, slowly navigating the rough gravel roads leading up to the inviting A-frame house. One of the neighbors waved madly at me from her front yard.

"Yoo-hoo!" she called out as my old van without air conditioning crawled by with the driver's window down due to the suffocating early fall heat. "You must be staying at the Millers' place!"

"Yes," I called back. "I'm Carolyn, Jane's friend."

"Hello there. I'm Eleanor." Obviously quite a way on in her years, Eleanor hobbled toward the car.

"You've heard about the weather report, right?" She leaned into my window, steadying herself on my door. White curls had sprung loose from her messy bird's nest of a bun. She looked at me with the sharp eye of a bird as well. The wind had been blowing hairdryer hot all day, but by the time I had made the drive out to the remote beach, the trees were being tossed about like those in a Robert Frost poem. Eleanor sniffed the air.

"Tornado weather," she pronounced.

"Really?" I replied. "I mean, it doesn't seem stormy at all. Just hot and windy."

"Doesn't have to be stormy, hon," she said with a knowing nod. "There's been no electricity since lunch. It's out for miles. Besides, the radio just announced a tornado warning."

I looked glumly at my computer with its low battery in the passenger seat next to me.

"Great," I mumbled.

Here was the only forty-eight hours I've had to myself in over a decade of mothering and working—for a brief shining moment, there would be no children or students or engagements or even a husband—just me and my computer, a few books, a change of comfy clothes, and a bag of wonderfully me-centered groceries (including melting chocolate). I stared up at the windswept sky and listened to the roaring trees overhead, almost as deafening as the self-pity welling up as I asked myself the eternal existentialist question of every exhausted mother out there: *Why?* Or, more precisely, *why now?* Eleanor must have followed my dismayed gaze, because she piped up in commiseration.

"Oh you poor thing, aren't you that writer with all those kids? Jane talked about you coming to finish your book. And now you'll be sitting in the dark. But then again, maybe that'll be better for you, hon. You know, restful . . ." Eleanor chuckled.

I didn't feel like laughing.

"What are you writing?" Eleanor asked brightly.

"I write on the intersection of faith and literature," I announced automatically.

"Oh." Her crestfallen face filled my window.

"But . . ." I took a deep breath and added what could arguably be identified as an *embellishment*: "I also write racy things."

"Oh?!" She perked up, intrigued rather than disappointed now. "Do you write under a pseudonym?" she asked slyly.

I thought of my beloved Bronte sisters and nodded. Charlotte would be proud, I reasoned to myself. Maybe not Emily or Anne, but definitely Charlotte.

"The name of my new book," I leaned in closer to her, lowering my voice, "has *sex* in the title."

"No!" she gasped, with shocked delight.

"*Yes*," I purred back.

"*Do* tell me more." White-haired Eleanor giggled like a schoolgirl.

I thought to myself how most novels (or films, for that matter) nowadays seem to simply connect the dots between sex scenes. It's all so, well, *predictable*. It's boring and condescending. Bestselling books always seemed to portray sex as panting and sweaty, and I honestly thought I might scream if I read one more time such phrases as "his manhood bulged" or "she heaved her breasts." Where was the ambience, the ache, the *delight*? The simple lowering of the shade in the carriage scene of Anna Karenina with Count Vronsky says more than a million booties shaking in one's face. The problem with this day and age is its reiteration of the obvious. Give me the mystery of the way of a man with a maid, or the epic and enduring love of an Odysseus and Penelope—with a bed lovingly carved out of olive, marking strength, peace, and fidelity, and the transformation of old lovers into young by the touch of a goddess's hand! Of eternal adoration, the Romantic Irish poet Thomas Moore wrote to his wife:

Believe me, if all those endearing young charms,
　Which I gaze on so fondly today,
Were to change by tomorrow, and fleet in my arms, . . .
Thou wouldst still be adored, as this moment thou art,
　Let thy loveliness fade as it will,
And around the dear ruin each wish of my heart
　Would entwine itself fervently still.

Why do modern writers, as a general rule, have such little imagination when it comes to sex? But then again, art imitates life. Perhaps the abundant life, however, is far more imaginative—imaginative beyond our wildest dreams!

Mad handfuls, not bouquets!

And yet what had happened to all those handfuls strewn over so many years? All those wedding wreaths I painstakingly made from my dried engagement flowers had crumbled away long ago. I wonder what Moore's wife thought, exactly, when she re-read his words later upon an anniversary? Here it was, almost my anniversary, and I was—alone—at a friend's cottage.

"Any marriage has times of separation, ill-health, or just plain crankiness, in which sexual intercourse is ill-advised," wrote Kathleen Norris. "And it is precisely the skills of celibate friendship—fostering intimacy through letters, conversation, performing mundane tasks together (thus rendering them pleasurable), savoring the holy simplicity of a shared meal, or a walk together at dusk—that can help a marriage survive the rough spots. When you can't make love physically, you figure out other ways to do it." Or, you don't. Without the great wind of inspiration, the Holy Spirit, our strings remain silent, our instruments untouched.

Tornado warning indeed.

"Carolyn?" I heard a voice toll me back.

"Yes?" I surfaced, slowly.

"Do tell!" Eleanor prompted me again.

"After the tornado, dear." I batted my eyes. Laughing, she patted my arm and stepped back so I could continue on my overheated way.

.ıllıllıı.

I have a confession. Yes, I had a manuscript deadline to meet. Yes, I had a massive pile of papers to grade. But I had also come to the cottage because my husband and I had a big argument. Well, let's make that big arguments, plural. Actually, it was more like a constant conversation of arguments, if conversation could be applied to one person yelling and the other yelling back.

I will not bore you, dear reader, with the details—other than life happens. And for most of us, at some point or another, life becomes downright "pretty shitty," as my poetics professor liked to reference as an example of feminine rhyme.

Unlike the little dilapidated cottage of my youth, this friend's cottage of my middle age was gorgeous. It sat nestled within pines a short walk across the private road to the beach. At the cottage's back rustled a forest, deep with trails and spotted by a few neighbors' private dwellings. The first time I entered the beautiful blue A-frame beside the equally blue Lake Huron, the architecture took my breath away. This was no cottage—at least not how I hitherto conceived of cottages. There were no raccoons to contend with on the front porch. No key on a hook above the door, where everyone in the vicinity knew it to be. No tiny rooms divided by curtains only, or a space heater for cold nights and a single fan for hot ones. No, this was a *lake house*—I would later joke with Jane about how she had deceived me in having referred to it as a *cottage*, so much so that I checked the address multiple times when I first drove up, and again even after I got the key to work in the lock.

Once inside, despite having rooms on multiple levels, the floorplan felt airy, given that the open stairs crisscrossed the living area to bedrooms in the middle of the house above so that most of the main floor still enjoyed high, vaulted ceilings. Floor-to-ceiling windows flanked three of the four walls in the back sitting room so that the outdoors seemed inside. This room quickly became my favorite as it overlooked the back forest, thick with birch, maple, and pine, all alive with the flitting birds of every size and color and song. It felt like sitting in a sanctuary, and I began to refer to it as such. I know that some of the most powerful writing has been produced in prisons, but I counted it a blessing to have this creative space more evocative of Samuel Taylor Coleridge's Lime-Tree Bower than Martin Luther King's Birmingham Jail or the Mamertine of Peter and Paul.

After unpacking my few things, I set my work down on the coffee table in the sanctuary and pulled up a comfortable chair. In the gloaming, I spied a lone raccoon scrambling down a gnarled, old tree in search of some nocturnal adventure. As I watched the sky slowly dim as evening came on, I realized that now, at this stage in my life, it was not the cottage that was dilapidated, but me.

With the power down all around, everything by nightfall went totally black and soundless. I lit a candle and inspected the fridge. It had grown warm, so I sadly ended up having to toss most of my gourmet groceries, another universal grief felt by mothers on rare retreat everywhere. I rooted around in the cupboard and found a can of tuna, which I opened for dinner and ate with the olives that were spared. There was no way to boil water for tea. I read part of a book I had brought, leaning close by the flame, but I found myself distracted. The screen had gone dead on my computer, and if the power didn't come on soon, my phone would be out of juice as well. Everything was rendered powerless, me most of all. Only the wind rushed mightily outside.

"Without Contraries is no progression," claimed William Blake in his famous long poem "The Marriage of Heaven and Hell." And indeed, marriage often feels that way: a progression through contraries, a regression of compromises, two steps forward and one step back. Depending on the dance, indeed of heaven or hell. In this quiet house, in the eye of the cyclone, this seemed a good time to stop moving myself, to slow down the dance. With Holy Spirit weather all around, this seemed a good place to sit within and be still.

.ılılılıı.

I awoke on my first morning to the alarm clock's blank face next to my bed: the power, to my dismay, was still down. I reached for my phone; its battery showed at less than a quarter. I had slept decadently late after all, given when my first child usually got up. The wind blew in angry gusts outside. I am an ambulatory thinker, and since I figured I would be journaling now instead of typing, I decided to try one of the trails as a way to work through my ideas. Maybe, too, the electricity would be on by the time I returned, and I could make a glorious cup of coffee!

I dressed quickly and stepped outside. Immediately the wind tore past me, blowing the screen door out of my hand and whipping my hair everywhere. Walking this morning was going to prove a challenge, I could already see. But I was determined not to be deterred. I decided to take the trail behind the house, leading southwest so that, like the Irish blessing, the wind would be at my back. The path wound between two neighboring cottages and then disappeared into the dense wood. The foliage formed a billowing canopy above me; the leaves rustled so loudly I could barely hear myself think. I felt sucked into the forest, lost in a vortex: the air moved so fast around me I could barely catch my breath. The branches groaned and cracked all around me, and just when I felt almost claustrophobic from the sylvan wind tunnel, the path took a sharp turn upward and I found myself cresting a sand dune.

All in a moment, the surging surf spread out before me. To my surprise, the trail had circled me back toward the lake, whitecapped with fury. If I had thought the wind through the trees was loud, that was nothing now compared to the thunderous crash of the waves. All of creation seemed to course with resounding power. The unpredictable tide rendered it too dangerous for me to walk the shore, so I stayed along the top of the shallow bluff, navigating my way through the brush and blowing sand. Losing track of time, I must have walked for hours, resting at various points along the way. Eventually I spotted another walkway up ahead, back into a thinner part of the woods. Completely disoriented by this point, I hoped that following a way where the trees were sparser would allow me to spot some sort of landmark to aid my way home. The battery on my phone flashed dangerously low, so I didn't want to use my navigation unless absolutely necessary. I also didn't want to yet admit I might need to.

Suddenly I stopped in my tracks. I heard it before I saw it: a distinct sweet tinkling sound, like silvered seashells shaken together. I knew that sound; I had heard it before, once, long ago. In a different life—far, far away.

A glint caught my eye through the heavy woods as I forced myself to continue on the path. It was indeed the silvered seashells moving against each other, threaded through by a fine chain. The windchime twisted wildly on the back porch of a house that looked strangely familiar. Yet I had never been here before. Or had I?

I created that windchime. Years ago, I collected those shells over the course of a summer along another lake. I carefully poked a whole at the hinge of each one, and then coated them with metallic paint. Once they dried, I painstakingly threaded each gleaming crescent through the links. The effect was a delicate but surprisingly strong ornament for making music from the breeze. When Ben and I were dating, I had given it as a gift to his parents one Christmas, hoping they might enjoy its music at the beach house they were building. They loved it and joyfully hung it outside the back door. The last time I was with Ben, it was just the two of us in the beach house still under construction, and we, too, were without power. We sat warming ourselves by the fire, eating a simple meal of bread, cheese, and wine. We talked, and then, when there was nothing more to say, we realized, fully, achingly, that we could not stay together. Unequally yoked, the yoke broke. Outside our window, in the winter wind, the silvery song played on.

I stood staring at the familiar yet unfamiliar house with the wind howling around me. *This must be another house. It cannot be this one,* I told myself.

But then it all began to make sense: the vaguely familiar name of the nearby beach community I had wandered towards, how the roads in the daytime now seemed evocative of some sort of dreamscape from long ago. When I looked back, I had only come to Ben's beach home in the dark. We would have driven the main road, entering by the main gate. In the winter, I wouldn't have traveled the other lane along the beach, the one I had taken yesterday. And I certainly had never walked the tangle of private trails behind the cottages before—not until today.

The branches cracked menacingly above me. I ventured closer to the house.

A beautiful chalet, it was finished now. The architecture was just as stunning—as unforgettable—as I remembered it. Ben's parents were people with a great appreciation for beauty and culture. His father had designed the house for his mother and built it mostly himself from his own designs. They planned to use it in their retirement, so he had worked lovingly on every detail.

Can it be? Is this the one? Stealthily, I circled the house, still remaining at a safe distance. I knew this was silly: I should walk by, remain unseen, mind my own business. But I was curious. Eve-like curious. Deadly curious.

The windchimes madly beckoned from the porch, tossed into a frenzy by the high winds.

And that's when I saw it: I stopped in my tracks for the second time. Surrounded by such a swirling surplus of air, I found myself unable to breathe. There. It. Was.

The truck. Ben's old truck, as distinctive as his parents' individualized beach house plans, sat parked to the side. Its headlights and the front fender, with the dents in all the right places, looked right at me with the face of an old friend.

What if he's here? I caught myself thinking while glued to the spot. *I should go.*

Should I stay?

Somehow I couldn't move—so I decided to stay. Then I reasoned: *Maybe I should say hello?* Suddenly a tide of thoughts broke loose:

What if everything's changed? What if it hasn't? You're being ridiculous ... you are being human ... it's entirely human to think about how an ex is doing ... It's not very Christian—hand to the plow, you know ... Well, it's very Christian to want to extend forgiveness, to ask for forgiveness, to desire closure ... No, it's dangerous ... no, it's valid ... no, it's an excuse ... What if someone else simply bought the truck with the house? Yes, that's it. And they kept the windchimes as part of the deal. There. No, that's even more ridiculous. Keeping a now very old truck, and a hokey craft to boot? What if his wife is there? What if his children are? Or, what if they are not? Or he doesn't have any? Or, regardless, what if he, too, is here, alone?

I couldn't tell if the wind was rushing inside or outside of my head.

Why, oh why, do we never meet our exes when things are going well?

Without warning I felt a vibration that caused me to just about jump out of my skin. As I pulled my buzzing phone from my pocket, I noticed someone standing in the upstairs sliding patio door of the chalet. Like a stalker, I stepped quickly behind a patch of trees, and, like an idiot, I hid hunched over and read my text in the midst of a massive windstorm outside my ex's parents' beach retirement home: *Hey Caro! You've been on my heart all morning. How are you? Did you make it to your friend's cottage? How is the writing going?*

One of my dearest friends in Christ, like many of my sisters in Christ, owned impeccable timing when it came to checking up on me. I have found that people of the earthly city are less likely to, while I have found that people of the city of God, however, take such "uncanny timing" as a matter of course. In fact, they find nothing "uncanny" about it at all; they actually seem expectant when I make this observation, or even, if I'm honest, uncannily secure. *Blessed assurance* indeed: such an inconvenient truth.

Okay. I texted back and left it at that.

A minute later my screen lit up: *Where are you?*

Shoot.

My phone battery signal was blinking with a red vengeance by now; I could practically feel the phone wilting in my hand. I wasn't sure what I felt more: concern at the battery dying or relief that it was.

My battery is about to go, I replied, truthfully.

I don't know if she was being Holy Spirit persistent or had simply hit resend, or if it was both, but the words *Where are you?* shot back at me again.

This was one of my closest friends—the walk-through-the-fire-with-you kind of friend. I took a deep breath and texted her as much of an explanation as I could tap out, as quickly as possible. Since she knew virtually everything about my life—past and present—and could easily fill in the gaps, the battery-countdown version didn't take long.

I hit *send* and waited. As branches crashed down around me, I hunkered down lower. It's a good thing I had my phone on vibrate, as the windstorm remained so noisy I couldn't have heard an alert.

Caro, I'm going into a work meeting here shortly. Will be able to read but can't reply easily. Tell me more.

I did.

I'm praying for you, she replied.

In a meeting? I responded.

Yes.

Not out loud, I hope, I tapped back.

You can pray anywhere, anytime, anyway, silly. I could practically hear my friend's dear voice.

I know. I tend to forget that.

I know. Are you praying, Caro?

Silence from me. Then: *No.*

I put the phone in my pocket and continued to watch the figure in the upper window through the brambles. I couldn't make out if it was a man or a woman.

After more silence, I felt the vibration again. My friend's words glowed again, too: *What are you doing now?*

Unsure, I tapped back: *Standing here.*

Why?

Thinking of knocking on the door.

Why? she asked.

Why not?

Silence.

More silence.

Just when I wondered if my phone had finally gone dead, it buzzed my palm.

Two words, in caps, stared back at me: *KEEP WALKING*

A moment later the screen went dead.

Another glint caught my eye as I turned my phone over in my hand. The diamond on my ring finger reflected the faint sunlight, and despite all those years of making meals, doing laundry, and washing dishes, of cleaning and caretaking and creating, it still sparkled like, well, the Christmas star. I stared at it for a long time. Then, leaving the chalet door un-knocked, I turned around and entered the unnavigated woods by a different route, all the while soundlessly praying my way home.

The shadows lengthened as the storm winds grew. Finally my own cottage came into view. Once safely inside, I threw myself on the couch. Thanks to my friend in Christ, I had walked on. Pain often makes any alternative look better than the current state by comparison; the hardest thing to do is to walk on through it. And it's impossible to walk all the way through it alone.

People say such events, like convenient interruptions or sudden provisions, are contrived, akin to the plot of a Dickensian novel. But Christians don't "see" things that way at all. Rather, they get the importance of story: they get the "plot." As an English teacher, I know that foreshadowing is one of the most effective literary devices in plot. Foreshadowing prepares us for what is to come: it can be a warning or a comfort, terrible or joyous. Or all of these at once. The Bible itself, from Genesis to Revelation, through prophecy and promise, operates according to foreshadowing, anticipating the final fulfillment.

I closed my eyes on the couch. *Just for a moment,* I reasoned to myself. My mind wandered over the years, over promises, over plots, finally coming to rest on my father's final words: "Life doesn't go as planned."

But you show up. As the saying goes, the first step to success is showing up. What happens, however, when one of you seems not to have shown up? Not showing up: that's what I literally experienced at our engagement party in Oxford, before we were to leave for our new life together in the States. Was that a foreshadowing? Of him? Of me? Of Christ? Of praying my way through the dark woods?

Hanging on to hope can be the hardest thing to do. Sometimes being in relationship means having hope rope burn.

Lying on that couch in my friend's cottage years after that party, moments after my prayer "walk on," I had to agree that at times in marriage hope can seem more akin to a slippery slope on an uphill climb than a jaunt through flowery fields. There are days I think of that first climb together on that tourist-free mound, and wonder: *Will we ever see the promised land?* And then I counter-wonder still: *Should it matter?*

A few years after our proposal scene, British Health and Safety declared the New College mound unsafe and therefore off limits after a drunken undergrad tumbled down the side and chipped a tooth. A group of students, saddened at the loss of a historically significant snogging spot amidst the shrubbery, formed a protest, demanding repair and access. Such are the battles at Oxford. Life, indeed, doesn't go as planned, but that doesn't mean there isn't a plot.

Slope. Rope. Hope. The masculine rhyme in the climb wasn't lost on me either.

"Yoo-hoo!" a now familiar voice shrilled through the screen door. "You okay in there, hon?"

Eleanor, my neighbor, had followed virtually on my heels, toting a canvas bag. I waved her in and she joined me on the couch.

"I thought you might be running low on candles with the power having been out for so long. I'm sorry I couldn't find a working flashlight."

"I'm sorry I can't offer you a cup of tea." I smiled back. "It was kind of you to pop over."

"I did just about kill myself getting here, if I'm honest."

"Eleanor, you shouldn't have walked here." I scolded her, immediately thinking that even the short distance down the road posed a challenge to her arthritic frame.

"Oh my knees were the least of my concerns, sweetheart." She patted my arm. "It was those gigantic trees in that wild wind! I kept waiting for one to come crashing down at any time, or, at the very least, for a heavy branch to knock me on the noggin. Now wouldn't that be a pretty sight—me spread-eagle in my dirty dungarees in the very elegant North Beach Pines!"

North Beach Pines—yes, that was it—the name of this little, quietly prestigious community of summer houses. Modest Jane never referred to it by name. But I remember now.

"Well, I better get back to Bert or he will wonder if the wind swept me up and carried me off—you know, like Mary Poppins." Eleanor giggled to herself at the joke. Then she pulled a loaf of homemade bread and a jar of peach preserves out of her bag.

"I keep a secret stash for times such as these." She smiled at me.

"Thank you," I said, deeply touched by the thoughtful gesture. "I will walk you back."

"No need, no need," Eleanor insisted, waving away my arm. "No need for two of us to get bumped into oblivion. I'll pop by tomorrow to check on you."

I was about to open my mouth to assure her there was no need for that either, but I could see for Eleanor that there was.

"Thank you," I said instead. "I look forward to it."

After Eleanor left, I made myself a generous plate of sliced bread with jam. The simple repast tasted delicious and so I gobbled a good half of it in one go. I hadn't realized until then just how hungry I was.

I also hadn't realized just how lucky I had been. Completely unawares, I had walked for miles through a densely wooded area in the worst windstorm in the area in decades, and I had emerged unscathed. I do not recall so much as a leaf touching me.

Through the kitchen window, as I licked peach preserves from my fingers, I marveled at the massive trees bending like reeds in the still growing gale. By candlelight, I mounted the stairs, brushed my teeth, and climbed into the comfortable bed. As I blew the flame out, I wished for healing for my marriage. Healing for *us*. The great wind seemed to have snuffed the stars from the sky in accordance with my wish. The cottage creaked like a galleon tossed at sea. I could hear small branches bounce off the roof above me.

But tree, I have seen you taken and tossed,
And if you have seen me when I slept,

You have seen me when I was taken and swept
And all but lost.

I feared that a fallen tree would crush me in my bed. Eventually, however, my eyes grew heavy, and, in spite of myself, my body relaxed into the welcoming sheets. I was too tired to fight, too weary to worry. I had no choice but to be carried. The storm circled chaos all around me, yet I slept.

Chapter Ten

ANNIVERSARY SONG

For the possession of goodness is by no means diminished by
being shared with a partner either permanent or temporarily
assumed; on the contrary, the possession of goodness is
increased in proportion to the concord and charity of each
of those who share it. In short, he who is unwilling
to share this possession cannot have it; and he who
is most willing to admit others to a share of it
will have the greatest abundance to himself.

St. Augustine

Very early in the morning, when the sky barely blushed with dawn, I woke to everything electrical in the house coming to life. Whirs and clicks and swooshes all happened at once as the power surged back on, I realized groggily. I tried to fall back to sleep, so rare was a lie-in, as the Brits would call it, with young children. To my irritation, however, something kept beeping downstairs; some sort of appliance or alarm required resetting. I would have to venture out of my cozy bed to see what it was. By the time I discovered and addressed the source of the sound down in the basement, I knew going back to sleep would be elusive, so I plugged my phone in its charger and put on a pot of coffee. Then I settled into my favorite seat in the sanctuary to watch the sky bolden into day over the treetops. The wind had quieted down completely now and gold finches flickered everywhere, along with one big, bossy blue jay.

Oh my love, I am sorry.

There was a time when dreams were green and energy was boundless, when I heard a woman speak of how she once bought her husband a very romantic anniversary card. She had selected it carefully, taking her time to open and read each one in the specialty stationary store's copious collection. She finally landed on the perfect card: the one with the meaningful image on its front, and that, once opened, bared exactly her own soul's feelings toward her beloved. She paid the price, far heftier than her usual purchase of a card for a special occasion might involve, and took the card home. There, she added her own terms of endearment to the inside message, followed by her signature. She sealed the envelope, addressing it to her husband. Then she slipped the card into her treasure box of special things she kept on top of her dresser. She didn't take it out again for a long, long time.

Had she simply forgotten to give it to him? Or was it lost in the stack of mementos, hidden among photos and letters, somehow just out of reach from even the most frenzied search?

No. It lay dormant with purpose—like hope caught fluttering under the lid of Pandora's box after all the evils had flown.

She and her husband were separated when she purchased the card. The silence between them had grown stony and thick; any communication that did happen between them only took moments to fragment into argument. They rarely touched and neither could remember the last time they'd had sex. Their lives clicked by in unison with the busyness of things: yes, they were a "good team" lovingly raising children, feeding children, and driving children to various things; paying bills and meeting commitments; attending fundraisers and potlucks and medical appointments; taking care of elderly parents and sick friends; adopting pets and serving in church; participating in councils, meetings, school events, and holidays—teaching, coaching, traveling, tidying. Together, they covered a lot of ground. Together, however, they got nowhere. Together, each was lost, alone.

It had gotten to such an oubliette of despair that the one insisted on marital counseling. The other reluctantly came along. Both felt alone, un-listened to, targeted, and invisible. Each resented the other. Each felt duped by the other: surely this was not the person the other had married? And because both were Christians who were committed to remaining married, or committed to the commitment, each felt trapped by God.

When, finally, there was nowhere left to go, the woman decided to pray. She prayed alone. At times she and her husband even prayed together. But she finally decided to pray proactively for him, and for their marriage, and for healing, and for her eyes to be open to what she could change, and for the gift of wisdom, and of love, and of grace, and of a peace surpassing all understanding. For years she prayed, until she became the prayer.

"I purchased the card as an act of complete trust between me and God," she explained, as I listened to her story on the radio, driving home late one night, alone in the dark. She knew her marriage was in a desperate place, and she had no idea how it would be saved. But she prayed. And she bought the card with the full trust in her heart that one day she would give it to her husband and mean every word it said. She didn't feel the words represented her current reality. She didn't feel the card was deserved. She didn't even know how she could ever be in the place to open it again. But buy and sign and treasure it away for the harvest of hope, she did.

"That card was as much for God as it was for my husband and me, perhaps even more," she claimed. It sat in that box for many a day, and night, and even more days, and even more nights. Until it would be easy, if not understandable, to think of it as forgotten or misplaced. But it wasn't. Whenever the woman despaired of her marriage, she thought of that card. And she trusted that her God would provide her the occasion to give it.

And in time, in his time, in *kairos* time, he did.

It is easy to look at others and think they have everything squared away. That they have things easier or better. That they live charmed lives, lives with every convenience or fewer burdens to bear. But this kind of judgment hurts our own hearts, which is why there is a commandment against it. When Jesus tells the men who are about to punish the accused woman, "You who has not sinned, cast the first stone," they all file away, one by one, until the only one who hasn't sinned is left alone with the woman. Though entitled, Jesus casts no stone, and speaks only words of release into peace: "Go, and sin no more." He unhooks the hooker, so to speak. He casts and catches and releases us into perfect freedom, which brings our own will, and thereby dignity, in accordance with God's. Fishers of men, and women, indeed. Walker of water, calmer of storms, prince of peace.

"God does not save us from temptations; He succours us in the midst of them," wrote Oswald Chambers, citing Hebrews 2:18. "Because he himself suffered when he was tempted, he is able to help those who are being tempted." In marriage, not only are two bodies joined, but so are two minds and two temples. "Have we recognized that our body is the temple of the Holy Ghost?" Chambers continued. "If so, we must be careful to keep it undefiled for Him. We have to remember that our conscious life, though it is only a tiny bit of our personality, is to be regarded by us as a shrine of the Holy Ghost. He will look after the unconscious part that we know nothing of; but we must see that we guard the conscious part for which we are responsible."

A wise friend of mine in Christ reminds me to pray that God will redeem our suffering. There is so much suffering, most of which goes unseen, or so we think. St. Augustine reminds us of a meaning we cannot (yet) fully grasp behind the truth that "God had one son on earth without sin, but never one without suffering."

How many of us live with an anniversary card secreted away in our box of treasures? How many of us trust that it will be opened, that the inscription to the beloved will be revealed in God's time? How many of us believe that in heaven we will be who we were made most perfectly to be? And that others will be made in that image of perfection fully realized into the really real as well? Sometimes, perhaps, marriage runs relatively smoothly overall, given the fallen nature of things. But for most, and for those married the longest, it is learned that you have to fight the devil for your marriage. You have to dig around in the rubble for the remnant of your noble selves. And then, with God's help, together you build a new temple.

.ılıllıı.

Marriage is the only human relationship based on an oath. Two people promise to love one another, till death do they part. We make no such promises with birthed or adopted children, with extended family, with friends, with coworkers, or with neighbors. In fact, we do not "promise" to love anyone like we promise to love a spouse. The covenant of marriage, therefore, differs greatly from just the joining of two people who happen, at the moment, to like one another. As Michael Coogan explains, in the Judeo-Christian tradition "marriage was a contract—the Hebrew word is *berit,* used mostly for the contract or covenant between God and Israel—between a man and the father of the bride-to-be, and also between husband and wife." A contract is a promise, in good faith. A commitment between two parties with witnesses. An agreement to keep your end of the bargain. To honor another, and in doing so, honor God. As the famous American author Nathaniel Hawthorne wrote to his wife, Sophia, in response to her fear if he would still love her in their old age: "Yes," Hawthorne penned, "you will be the same to me, because we have met in Eternity, and there our intimacy was formed." No wonder there are few griefs that cut more sharply, if we are honest with ourselves, than divorce.

No wonder, then, too, that Jesus' very first miracle happens at a wedding celebration, and it is literally a "taste and see that the Lord is good" moment. "On the third day a wedding took place . . ." I love the symbolism of the Bible. It is more beautifully intricate and interconnected than any other text by far. This would be the third day after Jesus' baptism by John the Baptist, foreshadowing Jesus' resurrection on the third day after the crucifixion. This story, like all stories in the Bible, opens up into multiple meanings like a set of Russian dolls. Fathomless, as Madeleine L'Engle described the Bible, in that we can never ever plumb its full depths. So we know, then, that this story tells of an ordinary wedding and yet it is no ordinary wedding. The wedding on the third day also points to our personal marriage to Christ in our resurrected lives and to the communal marriage of the Bride (or church) to the Bridegroom (or Christ). This later heavenly relationship will be the ultimate marriage, the one toward which our earthly relationship points. Again, foreshadowing points toward full light.

The wine we taste now is nothing compared to the wine we will taste later. With aging in Christ comes the fullness of time, and with the fullness of time into the eternal comes God's wisdom. I find it interesting that the servants fill the jars to the brim. The word *servants* suggests not only the waiters at the wedding banquet, but also the servants of Christ, or those who bring the blood of his body—the wine of communion—to others who thirst for the truth and the life. The jars are filled to the very top, just as God's graciousness overflows and his mercy rolls like a river.

"Give, and it will be given to you. A good measure, pressed down, shaken together and running over, will be poured into your lap. For with the measure you use, it will be measured to you." Like the over-pouring, Jesus isn't skimpy in his miracle either. Like the loaves and the fishes, he makes, well, *a lot* of wine. There is more than enough for the guests. No one is meted out a small taste, but rather gallons and gallons of water are transformed into the precious drink. This is an instance of where *in vino veritas* is indeed "in wine there is truth." The truth is in the taste of the living water, of the blood of the lamb. So much so that even the master of the banquet congratulates the bridegroom on not only the quality of the wine but also on the timing of its provision. The master appreciates the miracle even though he was not directly witness to it. And that makes all the difference, for the difference between Eden and heaven is appreciation: not only the understanding of value but also the recognition of how knowledge becomes wisdom with time and experience.

Jesus' miracle here is also his gift to the bride and groom, and the Bride and Groom, because he displays just how investment increases appreciation. We can only gain the "good wine" by running the good race, by remaining faithful and true. As in earthly marriage, we taste the "best wine" by enduring the test and gaining the wisdom of time. That is why a man leaves his father and mother and is united with his wife, and they become one flesh. Marriage, the greatest of all investments, is not unlike smaller ones, such as a mutual fund or real estate; you need to ride out the bumps, the highs and the lows, the richer and poorer, the sickness and health, and grow in trust and appreciation. Then, and only then, does the investment eventually—eternally—pay off. Again, marriage shows us how the earthly template anticipates the heavenly one.

I remember Jesus' final taste of bitter agony on the cross, the sponge dipped in vinegar and placed against parched lips. I must remember, then, too, the promise that even the most forgotten and condemned will be remembered in paradise – in life, the kingdom is always at hand, and in death, its entrance lies merely a heartbeat away. I must trust in the winemaker.

.ıllıllıı.

My phone, now charging, buzzed against the table. It was my husband, checking in despite our argument because he was worried about the power still being out and the phone possibly dead. It was the second time in less than twenty-four hours that merely two words illuminated my screen but said so much: *I'm sorry.*

Soon, it would be sunset. The storm had passed by my door. *Red sky at night, sailor's delight.* The horizon burns with time. In God's time, bitter *will* become better; the dirty slough will be a cleansing sea. Marriage weathered in Christ will roll around delightfully on the tongue like a fine wine. And perfect love will cast out fear.

I packed my few belongings quickly, sweeping up my keys in my eagerness to get home. Shortly after I pulled away from the lakeside cottage, I had to smile at the Cowboy Junkies' "Anniversary Song" playing on the radio: *Have you ever seen a sight as beautiful as a face in a crowd of people that lights up just for you?*

I took the road less traveled home, following the shoreline as long as I could. The water, now calm, spanned endless and aflame with the glory of God.

AFTERGLOW

Scripture begins in a garden but ends in a city.

HERBERT HAROLD KENT

About a month after my father passed away, I was clearing messages from my phone. Among them I discovered a voicemail my father had left shortly before his fatal fall. Somehow it had been overlooked and had gone straight to saved messages (I find myself smiling even now at God's good puns). Here is the message my father left, clear as a bell in mind and voice: "Hi honey. Just wanted to tell you I'm doing fine, and I love you very much. I hope you have a good trip. Tell that wonderful husband of yours that I love him. Thank him for teaching me about Jesus. I know that I am loved and that God is with me; he has always been with me. Thank your husband for helping me learn what it is to be a good dad. Goodbye, sweetheart." I never could have seen that birthday gift coming, so long ago. But the Unseen did.

"Now here is my secret," wrote Antoine de Saint-Exupery. "It is very simple. It is only with one's heart that one can see clearly. What is essential is invisible to the eye." Learning to properly "order our loves" after having disordered them through the fall is how St. Augustine identified the pilgrimage through grace. This not only involves, then, how best to love, but also who first to love so that everything else falls lovingly into place. The joy of a companion in Christ reflects our Savior's love for each of us, unequaled and unlike any other force that exists. Soon, we will be face to face with God who knows us best and loves us most.

Marriages may fail, but God's design and intention for them does not. Moreover, one does not need to be married, of course, in our earthly life in order to be married to Christ. Quite the opposite, as marriages can become idols just as easily as anything else. Putting God first is so important and fundamental to everything that follows that it composes the very first commandment.

Once I heard an interview with the rock star Bono in which he asked why doesn't anyone write a book about what marriage is *really* like—about the real shit that happens in marriage, including a marriage of faith? He and his wife, teenage sweethearts from Ireland, have been married for thirty-eight years and counting. They have obviously faced their storms of struggle and stardom, raising four well-adjusted children out of the spotlight while navigating their own sins and desires of the heart.

Sheldon Vanauken, in his enduring memoir *A Severe Mercy,* tells the story of his courtship, marriage, and then the untimely death of his wife, Davy. He compares sex before and after marriage as they both converted to Christianity at separate points after their marriage. He also shows the privilege and the pain, the unspeakable joys and the heartrending responsibilities, of growing in Christ next to someone with whom the ties of the body secure, too, the ties of the soul.

A very wise old woman in Christ once told me how in her long life of counseling married couples, she had never once seen a couple in which the two people were not equally matched in their short-comings. God puts people together so that they can work in grace for the sum to be greater than their parts. One might think the other needs fixing, but they are more than likely equally matched in their problems, albeit they may be of a different sort. The physical template in which a husband and wife fill each other's gaps anticipates the spiritual one. Like Rocky Balboa famously said about his wife, Adrian: "She's got gaps, I've got gaps, together we fill gaps."

The older I get, the more convinced I become that sex is the early Gorilla Glue of marriage. It then becomes the touchstone for remembering what it is to be remembered, and what it is, both physically and emotionally, to enter another person, to become one with them—their fears, secrets, worries, dreams, and hearts' desires. We experience that blind, crazy, intoxicating initial attraction, I think, so as to pull the magnets together that later we must learn to keep together ourselves. Sexual attraction becomes the seedbed of spiritual discipline. Forgiveness is spiritual heroism. Is there any greater answer to longing than to be fully known?

.ıllıllıı.

"The truth is that there has never been a very close match between human instincts and Judeo-Christian sexual morality," concluded Reay Tannahill at the very end of her bestselling tome *Sex in History*.

I'll say. But isn't that the Bible's point? As I wrote this book in my hometown of London, Canada, the Ontario government implemented a new sex education curriculum in the public school system. In the backdrop of my thoughts percolated the concerns for my own children. I guess it is much like Augustine's mom, Monica, praying without ceasing for her son to know the God who loves us beyond reason and understanding. We talk to our children about having "protected" sex but not about protecting their hearts. We don't set examples for their bodies as temples of the Holy Spirit. Growing up, I wish I had been given the knowledge of God's great love for me. I could weigh it and dismiss it if I so chose, but I could also implement it and all such a concept holds. What are we afraid of, especially in the walls of our schools, that we do not give our children such rudimentary knowledge? Nor the dignity to decide for themselves?

And so this book is the product of my giving serious thought as to what I would like to tell my own children about what relationship means to those who live in the city of God. Their father, TDH (Tall, Dark, and Handsome), who is now TBH (Tall, Bald, and Handsome), offers proof of how one good man does indeed change the world—for generations to come. And yet for all of its foreshadowing and fore-tasting, a marriage of two imperfect people is in no way a substitute for, or detraction from, our First Love who loves each of us perfectly.

"The sexual intercourse of man and woman, then, is in the case of mortals a kind of seedbed of the city," wrote Augustine. "But while the earthly city needs for its population only generation, the heavenly needs also regeneration to rid it of the taint of generation." This wide, troubled, lost world—for all its remnants of beauty, its reminders of joy—will murder and wound and steal. The only antidote, the only hope, I remind my children, is to cling to God with all they are worth, to always remember who they are, to never allow anyone or anything —in other words, any idol—to take their hearts away from their first love in God. For where their treasure is, their hearts will be also. Such treasure enriches all decisions they make through their hearts.

With the knocking at the hospital counseling room door that stormy October afternoon, my world shifted. And after all the decisions, I eventually found myself alone with my father, who lay dying. As his breathing slowed, I thought back to one of my dearest wishes as a little girl: that I would have traded everything for a close relationship with my father. To be utterly, completely, and unfailingly loved. I thought of all those birthday wishes, breathed by each of us, throughout the stories of our lives.

And then in those final moments, there we sat. Alone but together. Holding hands.

"Now faith is confidence in what we hope for and assurance about what we do not see." In the days that poured in between that first pounding at the cottage gate, my tentative knocking at the Bible study entry, and that final gentle rap at the hospital room door, I learned how obedience gives us eyes to see in the dark.

Why is it we never think of the far-reaching ramifications of sex? Why is it that we do not think of the fact that whom we share our living bed with most likely determines who will be at our deathbed? Or whom we ourselves might end up being on it? It would seem that the long-ago twinkle in my father's eye diamonded the tears falling from mine. There is not one of us through this wide world who is unbound by the intricate web of intimate relationship. There is not one of us who does not bear the image of another. Just as there is not one of us without sin, there is not one of us not made in the image of God. Just as there is not one of us justified in casting the first stone, there is not one of us who does not long to go in peace.

The picture of me at the cottage during my seventh birthday now sits in a frame next to our marriage bed. At the end of many a long day, I hold it close and see anew, see now, the radiant joy of a daughter whose father's good pleasure it is to give her the kingdom.

⸱⸱ıⅠⅼⅠⅼıⅼⅰ⸱

TBH says many a wise and witty thing, but there are two that I wish to leave with you here. These are refrains of his I can count on when

I've failed or been rejected or simply had a bad day. First, he holds me tight and looks me in the eye and says, "That's when you get extra luvs." The phrase never ceases to make me smile. The second is when he reminds me, with his charmingly wry, lopsided grin, "Well, babe, there's always eternity."

"But there is not now space to treat of these ages;" Augustine concluded, "suffice it to say that the seventh shall be our Sabbath, which shall be brought to a close, not by an evening, but by the Lord's day, as an eighth and eternal day, consecrated by the resurrection of Christ, and prefiguring the eternal repose not only of the spirit, but also of the body. There we shall rest and see, see and love, love and praise."

Sex in the city of God reminds us that there is an eternity of extra luvs. Amen.

ACKNOWLEDGMENTS

I wish to thank and acknowledge privately in my own heart those whose marriages in Christ have inspired me, and those who have also treated their sexuality (regardless of relationship status or orientation) as a means by which to glorify God. Sex, like all things God made and deemed good, is, too, a paradox (or *seeming* contradiction) that has little to do with the act itself and more to do with the human heart that perceives it. I particularly wish to thank a mentor couple in our church: Jen and Brent Paul, for taking us under their wings and being available as Christ is available in gentle, persistent, loving ways. I also wish to thank Jon and Darlene Korkidakis, our pastor and his wife, for their Greek hospitality in opening, always without hesitation, their home, hearth, and hearts to us. As Jon says about following Jesus and shining your light to others in need: when in doubt, better to err towards the generous. I have found this adage is a good one to live by in marriage too.

Thank you to my dear sisters-in-Christ, who have read, edited, and offered suggestions and support (for my writing and my marriage and my sanity!): my dearest Tabitha Elwood for loving me across all the miles, Marianne Vanderboom for traveling with me in oh so many ways, Natalie Price for being such a place of safety and insight, and Nicole St. John for always being a text away and ready with the biggest heart in the world. Thanks to Jill Matsuo for her lake house hospitality; your generosity intersected with my want. Thank you to my sister, Kelly, incredible and dedicated wife and mother, and most of all, patient in the Lord. You have taught me much, little sister. You are all women who inspire me and have me shake my head in wonder that God would gift you to me.

Thank you to the team at InterVarsity Press, and particularly to Jeff Crosby and Cindy Bunch, for their immense support, personally and professionally. Thank you to my agent, Mark Sweeney, for always believing in and caring for Team Weber.

Thanks to my precious children for putting up with mommy's many distractions and for inspiring me to discern. Like my own mom always lovingly said to me, "Just wait until you have children, then you'll see."

Finally, my Kent, despite all the uncompressed dirt on this side of heaven, let's get on our sexy boots and sing Psalm 26 along with Bono: "Laughter is eternity if joy is real!" The other side is more beautiful than we can ever imagine; the fallen tips more toward the gracious than not. And so I am re-membered on that dance floor, you holding me, with God, forever: *Come with me, my love. To the sea— the sea of love. I want to tell you, oh how much, I love you.*

NOTES

PROLOGUE: IN ANTICIPATION

1   *Is it hubris*: Leif Enger, *Peace Like a River* (New York: Atlantic Monthly Press, 2001), 55.

1. SAVED SEX

13   *My grace is sufficient*: 2 Corinthians 12:9.

      They also serve who: John Milton, "When I consider how my light is spent," Sonnet 19, 1655, Poetry Foundation, www.poetryfoundation.org/poems/44750/sonnet -19-when-i-consider-how-my-light-is-spent.

14   *An awful tempest mashed the air*: Emily Dickinson, "An Awful Tempest," in *Winter Poems*, ed. Barbara Rogasky (New York: Scholastic, 1995), 39.

19   *Men who make do*: Joan Anderson, *A Year by the Sea* (New York: Doubleday, 1999), 24.

21   *Ah, love, let us*: Matthew Arnold, "Dover Beach," 1867, Poetry Foundation, www .poetryfoundation.org/poems/43588/dover-beach.

22   *Lord, I'm coming home*: Lynyrd Skynyrd, "Sweet Home Alabama," *Second Helping*, MCA, 1974.

32   *I will make you*: Matthew 4:19 ESV.

33   *My heart is like a singing bird*: Christina Rossetti, "A Birthday," Poets.org, poets .org/poem/birthday.

35   *have life, and have it*: John 10:10.

2. THE SINGULAR LIFE

40   *Disturb us, Lord*: Francis Drake, "Disturb us, Lord," c. 1577, https://pilgrimchurch prayers.wordpress.com/2016/01/13/disturb-us-lord-a-prayer-of-sir-francis-drake.

42   *I know what you mean*: G. K. Chesterton, *The Man Who Was Thursday* (n. p.: Merchant Books 1908, 2009), 112.

44   *Why have you come*: Fyodor Dostoyevsky, *The Brothers Karamazov*, trans. Ignat Avsey (Oxford, UK: Oxford University Press, 1994), 313.

46   *He who resolves to love*: St. Augustine, *The City of God*, trans. Marcus Dods (Peabody, MA: Hendrickson Publishers, 2009), 404.

      Verily, verily, I say unto you: John 12:24 KJV.

47   *upright heart and pure*: John Milton, *Paradise Lost* (New York: Longmans, Green, and Co., 1896), 5.

48   *My beloved spoke and said*: Song of Songs 2:10-12.

50   *Because I talk so much*: Mother Teresa, National Prayer Breakfast, Washington, DC, February 3, 1994, transcript at Crossroads Initiative, www.crossroads initiative.com/media/articles/mother-teresas-national-prayer-breakfast-message.

3. IT'S ALL RELATIVE

57   *the most reluctant convert*: C. S. Lewis, *Surprised by Joy* (New York: Harcourt Brace & Company, 1955), 221.

60 *Faithless is he that says*: J. R. R. Tolkien, *The Fellowship of the Ring* (Boston: Houghton Mifflin, 1954), 294.

61 *Of these two first parents*: St. Augustine, *The City of God*, trans. Marcus Dods (Peabody, MA: Hendrickson Publishers, 2009), 432.

62 *The first founder of the earthly city*: Augustine, *City of God*, 639.

63 *for we are members*: Ephesians 5:30.

    On each side of the river: Revelation 22:2.

64 *I am* in relationship *not just to*: J. Richard Middleton, *A New Heaven and a New Earth: Reclaiming Biblical Eschatology* (Grand Rapids, MI: Baker Academic, 2014), 22.

    shining barrier: Sheldon Vanauken, *A Severe Mercy* (New York: HarperCollins, 1977), 24.

4. Premarital Sects

68 *the brown brink eastward*: Gerard Manley Hopkins, "God's Grandeur," in *God's Grandeur and Other Poems* (New York: Dover Publications, Inc., 1995), 15.

71 *There are more things in heaven*: William Shakespeare, *Hamlet*, Act 1, Scene 5.

72 *Do not be yoked together*: 2 Corinthians 6:14.

73 *my yoke is easy*: Matthew 11:30.

    shining barrier: Sheldon Vanauken, *A Severe Mercy* (New York: HarperCollins, 1977), 24.

    The earthly city, which does not: St. Augustine, *The City of God*, trans. Marcus Dods (Peabody, MA: Hendrickson Publishers, 2009), 628.

74 *Ethics is lived eschatology*: J. Richard Middleton, *A New Heaven and a New Earth: Reclaiming Biblical Eschatology* (Grand Rapids, MI: Baker Academic, 2014), 24.

81 *Among twenty snowy mountains*: Wallace Stevens, "Thirteen Ways of Looking at a Blackbird," in *The Collected Poems of Wallace Stevens*, corrected edition, ed. John N. Serio and Chris Beyers (New York: Penguin Random House, 2015), 99.

83 *the ancient Persians debated everything*: C. S. Lewis, *Letters to Malcolm: Chiefly on Prayer* (New York: Harcourt and Brace, 1963), 45.

87 *The more you focus*: Sarah Young, *Jesus Calling* (Nashville: Thomas Nelson, 2004), 236.

88 *But I tell you*: Matthew 5:28.

90 *every snow crystal is hexagonal*: Robert Wild, *The Tumbler of God: Chesterton as Mystic* (Tacoma, WA: Angelico Press, 2013), 12.

    Nobody will know, when you're old: The Rolling Stones, "She's So Cold," *Emotional Rescue*, Atlantic Records, 1980.

91 *of cloudless climes*: Lord Byron, "She walks in beauty," 1813.

    We have something of God: Frederick Buechner, *Telling Secrets* (New York: Harper-Collins, 1991), 44.

5. On the Road

96 *You've got to know*: Kenny Rogers, "The Gambler," *The Gambler*, United Artists, 1978.

97 *Sometimes I think it's a shame*: Gordon Lightfoot, "Sundown," *Sundown*, Reprise Records, 1974.

101   *Sundown, you better take care*: Lightfoot, "Sundown."

109   *It's a question of denying*: Grace Irwin, *Least of all Saints* (Old Tappan, NJ: Fleming H. Revell, 1976), 171.

   For as, when the spirit: St. Augustine, *The City of God*, trans. Marcus Dods (Peabody, MA: Hendrickson Publishers, 2009), 387.

111   *Come to me*: Matthew 11:28.

116   *As usual, we put feeling first*: Hannah Whitall Smith, *The Christian's Secret of a Happy Life* (Berkeley, CA: Apocryphile Press, 2007), 19-20.

117   *And therefore it is that humility*: Augustine, *City of God*, 413.

   Where love is, God is: Henry Drummond, *The Greatest Thing in the World* (Grand Rapids, MI: Baker Books, 2011), 25.

118   *Clark Kent, now there was*: Crash Test Dummies, "Superman's Song," *The Ghosts That Haunt Me*, BMG/Arista, 1991.

   In the middle of the journey: Dante Alighieri, *The Divine Comedy*, Inferno Canto 1:1-60.

   Sometimes I despair the world: Crash Test Dummies, "Superman's Song."

119   *Death destroys a man*: E. M. Forster, *Howards End* (New York: Macmillan, 1997), 324.

120   *Life is always fatal*: This quote is often attributed to Peter Kreeft.

   like the do-dah man: Grateful Dead, "Truckin'," *American Beauty*, Warner Bros., 1970.

121   *Sometimes the light's all shinin'*: Grateful Dead, "Truckin'."

6. Guest Night

124   *Delight yourself in the Lord*: Psalm 37:4 ESV.

125   *A motion and a spirit*: William Wordsworth, "Lines Composed a Few Miles above Tintern Abbey, On Revisiting the Banks of the Wye during a Tour. July 13, 1798," Poetry Foundation, www.poetryfoundation.org/poems/45527/lines-composed-a-few-miles-above -tintern-abbey-on-revisiting-the-banks-of-the-wye-during-a-tour-july-13-1798.

   You shall have no other: Exodus 20:3.

126   *Do you not know*: 1 Corinthians 6:19-20.

129   *To raise bare walls*: Virginia Woolf, *A Room of One's Own*, annotated ed. (London: Harcourt, Inc., 2005), 23.

130   *You shall have*: Exodus 20:3.

131   *I do not give to you*: John 14:27.

133   *The world is charged*: Gerard Manley Hopkins, "God's Grandeur," in *God's Grandeur and Other Poems* (New York: Dover Publications, Inc., 1995), 15.

135   *God loves each of us*: This quote is often attributed to St. Augustine.

   And though the last lights: Hopkins, "God's Grandeur," 15.

136   *Faith is to believe*: This quote is often attributed to St. Augustine.

   Because the Holy Ghost: Hopkins, "God's Grandeur," 15.

7. Sweetness to the Soul

137   *An Aeronaut to His Love*: Witter Bynner, "An Aeronaut to His Love," in Miller Williams, *Patterns of Poetry* (Baton Rouge: Louisiana State University Press, 1986), 161.

142   *I feel pretty*: Leonard Bernstein, Stephen Sondheim, Arthur Laurents, "I Feel Pretty," *West Side Story*, original Broadway production, 1957.

144 *Have you met my good friend*: Bernstein et al., "I Feel Pretty."

146 *You always end with a jade's*: William Shakespeare, *Much Ado About Nothing*, Act 1, Scene 1.

Thou dost infect: William Shakespeare, *Richard III*, Act 1, Scene 2.

148 *I feel stunning*: Bernstein et al., "I Feel Pretty."

149 *Why? Sweet love*: Bynner, "An Aeronaut to His Love."

156 *It's like rain*: Alanis Morissette, "Ironic," *Jagged Little Pill*, Maverick, 1995.

159 *An Ode to Carolyn and Kent*: This poem was written in celebration of our wedding in October 1997 by two former English literature students of mine, Ben Arnoldy and Marney Parker. They gifted us with the framed poem, which still hangs on my wall today.

8. SEA OF LOVE

170 *Come with me, my love*: The Honeydrippers, "Sea of Love," *Volume One*, Atlantic Records, 1984; original: Philip Baptiste, *Sea of Love*, Mercury Records, 1959.

171 *There was a time when meadow*: William Wordsworth, "There was a time," in *The Miscellaneous Poems of William Wordsworth in Four Volumes* (London: Paternoster-Row, 1820), 275.

172 *Let the beloved*: Deuteronomy 33:12.

173 *extend our lives by one moment*: Luke 12:25, paraphrase.

When you are old: William Butler Yeats, "When you are old," 1892, Poetry Foundation, www.poetryfoundation.org/poems/43283/when-you-are-old.

Being in love: C. S. Lewis, *Mere Christianity* (New York: Macmillan, 1943, repr. 1978), 99.

174 *This will not be*: Joan Didion, *The Year of Magical Thinking* (New York: Knopf, 2005), 197.

Love is patient: 1 Corinthians 13:4-8.

Father, forgive them: Luke 23:34 ESV.

175 *Obedience is not so much*: Lucinda Vardey, *Word Made Flesh* (Toronto: Novalis, 2016), 30.

In Britain the Englishman is: Henry Drummond, *The Greatest Thing in the World and Other Writings* (New Kensington, PA: Whitaker House, 2017), 27.

Meaningless!: Ecclesiastes 1:1-2.

Through all this ordeal: G. K. Chesterton, *The Man Who Was Thursday* (New Kensington, PA: Whitaker House, 2014), 54.

176 *This is my body*: Luke 22:19.

The man and his wife: Genesis 2:25 NLT.

177 *What will become*: Delmore Schwartz, "Calmly We Walk Through This April's Day," in *Selected Poems 1938-1958* (New York: New Directions Publishing Corp., 1967), 66.

178 *I've conquered my past*: U2 with Bob Dylan, "Love Rescue Me," *Rattle and Hum*, Island Records, 1988.

9. THROUGH THE WOODS DARKLY

182 *Believe me, if all those*: Thomas Moore, "Believe Me, If All Those Endearing Young Charms," 1808, in *Love Letters*: ed. Rick Smith, *A Romantic Treasury* (Philadelphia: Running Press, 1996), 117.

Any marriage has times: Kathleen Norris, *The Cloister Walk* (New York: Riverhead Books, 1996), 118.

185   *Without Contraries is no*: William Blake, "The Marriage of Heaven and Hell," 1790.

194   *But tree, I have seen you*: Robert Frost, "Tree at my Window," in *West-running Brook* (New York: Henry Holt and Company, 1928), 25.

10. ANNIVERSARY SONG

199   *When Jesus tells*: John 8:1-11, paraphrase.

    God does not save: Oswald Chambers, *My Utmost for His Highest* (New York: Dodd, Mead & Company, 1935), 192.

    Have we recognized: Chambers, *My Utmost for His Highest*, 233.

200   *God had one son*: This quote is often attributed to St. Augustine.

201   *Marriage was a contract*: Michael Coogan, *God and Sex* (New York: Hachette Book Group, 2010), 69.

    Yes . . . you will be: Nathaniel Hawthorne, in *Love Letters: A Romantic Treasury*, ed. Rick Smith (Philadelphia: Running Press, 1996), 120.

    On the third day: John 2:1.

    Fathomless, as Madeleine L'Engle described: Madeleine L'Engle, *The Rock That Is Higher* (Wheaton, IL: Harold Shaw Publishers, 1993), 37.

202   *Give, and it will be*: Luke 6:38.

204   *Have you ever seen*: Cowboy Junkies, "Anniversary Song," *Pale Sun, Crescent Moon*, RCA/BMG, 1993.

EPILOGUE: AFTERGLOW

205   *Now here is my secret*: Antoine de Saint-Exupery, *Le Petit Prince* (Hertfordshire, UK: Wordsworth Editions, Limited, 1995), 82.

207   *She's got gaps*: *Rocky*, directed by John G. Avildsen (Beverly Hills, CA: United Artists, 1976).

    The truth is: Reay Tannahill, *Sex in History* (Chelsea, MI: Scarborough House Publishers, 1980, rev. ed., 1992), 432.

208   *The sexual intercourse*: St. Augustine, *The City of God*, trans. Marcus Dods (Peabody, MA: Hendrickson Publishers, 2009), 502.

    For where their treasure: Matthew 6:21, paraphrase.

    Now faith is confidence: Hebrews 11:1.

209   *to give her the kingdom*: Luke 12:32, paraphrase.

210   *But there is not now*: St. Augustine, *The City of God*, trans. Marcus Dods (Peabody, MA: Hendrickson Publishers, 2009), 781.

ACKNOWLEDGMENTS

212   *Laughter is eternity*: U2, "Get on Your Boots," *No Line on the Horizon*, Mercury/Interscope, 2009.

    Come with me, my love: The Honeydrippers, "Sea of Love," *Volume One*, Atlantic Records, 1984; original: Philip Baptiste, *Sea of Love*, Mercury Records, 1959.